I0071649

The Essential Guide for Network Marketing

Bryan J. Westra

Indirect Knowledge Limited
MURRAY, KENTUCKY

Copyright © 2013 by Bryan J. Westra.

All rights reserved. No part of this publication may be reproduced, distributed or transmitted in any form or by any means, including photocopying, recording, or other electronic or mechanical methods, without the prior written permission of the publisher, except in the case of brief quotations embodied in critical reviews and certain other noncommercial uses permitted by copyright law. For permission requests, write to the publisher, addressed "Attention: Permissions Coordinator," at the address below.

Bryan J. Westra/Indirect Knowledge Limited
2317 University Station
Murray, Kentucky/42071
www.indirectknowledge.com

Book Layout ©2014 Indirect Knowledge Limited

Ordering Information:
Quantity sales. Special discounts are available on quantity purchases by corporations, associations, and others. For details, contact the "Special Sales Department" at the address above.

Network Marketing/ Bryan J. Westra. —1st ed.

ISBN-10: 0989946479

ISBN-13: 978-0-9899464-7-6

Contents

*Dedicated to those serious about building a successful business
to be able to quit the 9 to 5!*

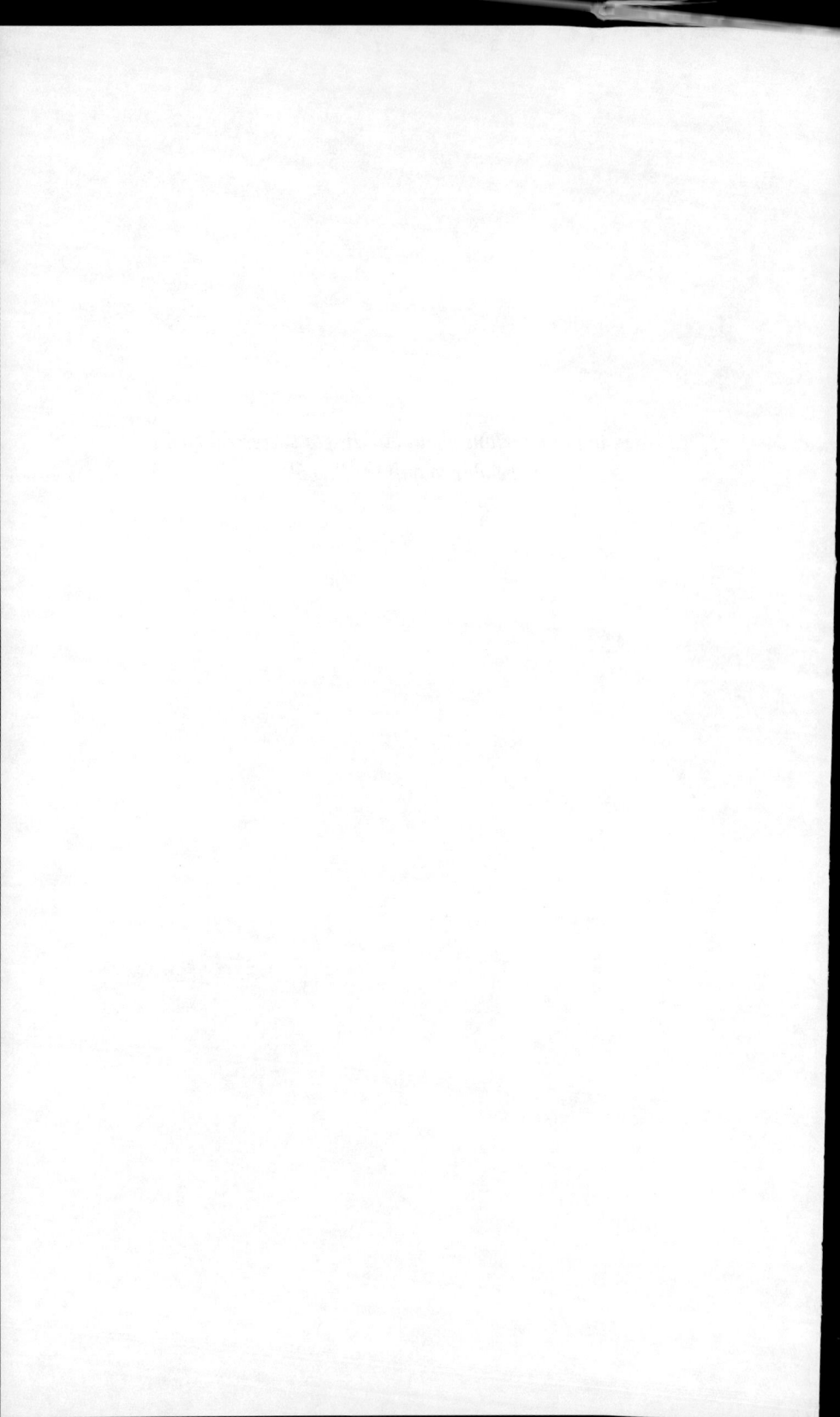

"I'm going to teach you the Law of Duplication; namely: What I'm going to teach you; I'm going to teach you to teach others."

—BRYAN WESTRA

DISCLAIMER

This book is designed to provide information and motivation to our readers. It is sold with the understanding that the publisher is not engaged to render any type of psychological, legal, or any other kind of professional advice. The content of each article is the sole expression and opinion of its author, and not necessarily that of the publisher. No warranties or guarantees are expressed or implied by the publisher's choice to include any of the content in this volume. Neither the publisher nor the individual author(s) shall be liable for any physical, psychological, emotional, financial, or commercial damages, including, but not limited to, special, incidental, consequential or other damages. Our views and rights are the same: You are responsible for your own choices, actions, and results. This book is designed to provide information on preaching and persuasion only. This information is provided and sold with the knowledge that the publisher and author do not offer any legal or other professional advice. In the case of a need for any such expertise consult with the appropriate professional. This book does not contain all information available on the subject. This book has not been created to be specific to any individual's or organizations' situation or needs. Every effort has been made to make this book as accurate as possible. However, there may be typographical and or content errors. Therefore, this book should serve only as a general guide and not as the ultimate source of subject information. This book contains information that might be dated and is intended only to educate and entertain. The author and publisher shall have no liability or responsibility to any person or entity regarding any loss or damage incurred, or alleged to have incurred, directly or indirectly, by the information contained in this book. You hereby agree to be bound by this disclaimer or you may return this book within the guarantee time period for a full refund.

INTRODUCTION

I was at the post office today and a girl at the counter got up the nerve to finally ask me: "What do you write about?" I suppose to most people it would seem rather mysterious, yet intriguing, that this rather ordinary looking guy gets these checks all the time coming in the mail, as well as him always sending off copies of books with his name on the cover.

This question sparked an interesting discussion. I told her I was just finishing up this book, the one you're holding in your hands, and that it was about Network Marketing, the industry, and an essential guide for network marketers.

She then said, "Been their; done that!"

I'm a master at reading body language and non-verbal cues and what fascinated me was the fact that when she spoke these words her face became illuminated and she was all smiles. This was, in my mind at least, incongruent with her words. I couldn't tell if she really secretly wanted to be in the industry of network marketing, or if she'd tried it, failed, and wanted nothing more to do with the industry.

Keep in mind this woman probably brings home a sizeable check. I had talked to a postal worker once who claimed that it was a great job, with great benefits, and one that most could retire from early enough in life to enjoy their mature years happily. I suspect by her personality that this young 20s something woman probably enjoys her job, as her attitude is usually helpful, and pleasant—more so than others in fact.

I didn't carry on about me and my writings and musings; yet, instead, I began to ask her clarifying questions to get more clearness about what she meant by what she had said.

The conversation remained on her the rest of our twenty minute conversation. In the end I had surmised that this young woman had tried her luck in network marketing before, had difficulty, failed –and, to my surprise still felt some regret getting out of the industry. It was as if she'd lost a part of herself, her values, her principles, and I might would argue, her sense of self-worth, when she went back to working a 9 – 5 at the post office.

As I walked out of the post office with my mail and packages, I somehow intuited that other people feel or have felt the exact same way.

This girl will not forget the journey she embarked on when she first made the decision to join a network marketing company with the intention of taking control of her financial destiny and to create the lifestyle dream she envisioned in her mind.

I'm not sure, by any stretch of the imagination, if this young woman will give network marketing a-go again, or not. I probably would guess, from our conversation, and how it ended, that she will find her way back.

Why do I share today's story with you in this introductory chapter? I do it because I want to introduce you to a problem that persists in this industry that has haunted me and other industry leaders for quite a long time. The problem effects you, as much as it does me.

The problem has to do with the little success most people have when deciding to become a network marketer. The problem goes like this: I'm a leader, I recruit people into my network marketing business frequently. I've been in the industry well over a decade. I recruit you, a new person.

You're excited. You want to make more money. You want not to have to listen to a boss tell you what to do anymore. You want to own nice things that only wealthy people can afford. You want to live a lifestyle that many commoners would judge as egocentric in nature. If you have a family, you want to spend more time with them; that is, watch your kids grow-up, or just be in their lives. To sum it all up...You want the dream.

Me, the leader, I want you to succeed. I want you to have all those things you desire. However, what I don't want is you leeching onto me, coming at me like I'm some savior, or guru that's here to help you—I'm not that person.

I'm just like you in many ways. I want the same things out of life you want. I put my pants on in the morning just like you. I may have a bigger house. I may have more money. I may have a bigger down line. I may have more the lifestyle you're seeking. But, I assure you, I'm no better than you, smarter than you, or the wise mentor you think I am.

In network marketing I cannot be that person and you be successful. The goal of network marketing is duplication. You have to be able to do exactly what I do. The system has to be proven to work for most anyone. It therefore has to be simple enough a child could replicate it without effort.

Back to the problem...

The problem is many new network marketers or those who begin tasting a hefty monthly residual income, forget this. They start to feed their egos as if they're somehow better or more qualified than you are. They're not!

The problem is really that I cannot baby you, or hold your hand, or motivate you, or make the sales for you, or work your business for you. Right now, you may be grimacing by what I tell you. But I'm not going to do you a disservice and lie to you. Other people will; but not I.

I've covered what you want from network marketing. I've told you the cold truth about the people in your up line who want to remain dissociated away from you, yet feel assured that you're working your business competently and consistently bringing in revenue for you, them, and the parent company you've decided to partner with. However, I haven't told you how I've solved the problem with this situation of you wanting the best training, and your up line wanting to forget about you, and continue doing the things that generate more income for them, which is selling the opportunity to more people, besides yourself.

See, let's look at this logically for a moment, as it will explain why this system of training is unsustainable. If I trained you after you joined my team, and spent my business hours with you, coaching you, helping you brand yourself, helping you market effectively to reach a target market, helping you to generate leads, and basically teaching you everything I know, I'd never be recruiting anyone; and neither would you. I'd in fact probably start to stress out, you would too, and soon the business model would fall apart.

But you still feel so convinced that I know so much while you know so little and that I possess some secret ingredient or resource that you don't have, and that I'm unwilling to share with you.

That's not the case. Unfortunately you're not the only person who feels this way. Most people, from my experiences, have shared with me that they thought I was holding back some key to the kingdom that would let them into some secret internet marketing club. Even so, let me reassure you, I nor anyone else in this industry possess any type of magic wand that ensures we're successful and you remain not.

Everyone above you in this network marketing company is secretly praying to some higher power that you will recruit the heck out of this opportunity and make us all rich. We're your biggest advocates, because we have the most to gain from your success. However, we still cannot be responsible for your success, because that's overkill for us. I mean, seriously, who wants to get phone calls at ten o'clock at night while they're watching their 90" television with their loved ones? I don't. I'm sure you don't either.

After all, the whole purpose of operating a network marketing business is to work less and make more money. All I really want to do is work my three hours per day calling on leads, selling my business opportunity to others, and to then go about the rest of my day doing whatever I want to do.

If you want the same, you're going to love this book. This book is written by a successful network marketer for network marketers. But who am I, and what makes me qualified to write this book, or to give you any advice whatsoever?

My name is Bryan Westra. I am a PH.D. Candidate in Counseling. I hold an MBA in Marketing. I hold a B.A. in Organizational Behavior and Sales Leadership. I have other specialized degrees in Psychotherapy, Hypnosis, and NLP. And in fact am a master practitioner and master level trainer in both Hypnosis and NLP. And, have even I've studied with the best trainers around the world. I've been a quiet superstar in network marketing for years, hiding outside the limelight of the industry.

Even though I can sell ice to Eskimos, make millions of dollars each year, and sell this book to you, I'm still, at the end of the day, just an ordinary guy, no different from anybody else. I wouldn't have it any other way.

But, and I hear you, I honestly do: "Why this book?" you ask? The reason you want this book is because it solves the age-old problem, not even Jim Rohn could quite articulate oh so well, which simply put is: How do I build a powerful down line in network marketing without struggling, or having to hand-hold, or do anything besides recruiting others into my organization –and, be able to make money? This book solves that problem. What would take your company a time to teach you, I can teach you in a good day. What your up line leaders can teach, I will teach you in this book. The answers and the solutions you plead others to give you, to hopefully make your life better, and your future secured in network marketing, I'm going to give you right here, right now, in this book.

Then I'm going to teach you the Law of Duplication and be a resource you'll use to build the strongest, most wealthy, down line, of expert network marketers the world has ever seen. All in the pages of this book!

The question I have to ask you, before you begin, is are you ready? By ready, I mean, are you ready to do EX-ACTLY what it takes to be successful? Are you willing to follow instructions to a 'T'? Are you coachable and traina-ble?

Right now is the deciding moment which will deter-mine whether you'll be successful or a failure. You must decide, before we get started, because I will hold you ac-countable for your decision. In other words, you must do exactly as I instruct you. No less.

So now, I've probably scared the crap out of you, or at least gotten your full attention. You've probably raised a red-flag or two and the warning bells are going off in your head. Let me assure you have nothing to be worried about. I'll ask nothing from you that isn't sane. I mean, like I said before, this has to be duplicable; that is, of course, this book has to be able to teach anyone to be a successful, and then teach their people as well.

Stay with me. You're going to love this journey!

Learn Well, Live Well,

Bryan J. Westra
www.indirectknowledge.com

CHAPTER 1

Ingredients

I Don't take shortcuts; for that reason, neither will you! Just like you're following a recipe to cook a fine dinner tonight for your significant other (To show them how much you appreciate and care about them!) the first thing you would do is grab your favorite cookbook, find the recipe you wanted to prepare, and then check to make sure you had all the ingredients listed for that particular recipe. This is step one. If you didn't have the right ingredients you'd then have two choices: (a) pick a different recipe, or (b) go to the store and purchase what you needed to prepare the meal.

This is something that sounds like common sense; however, you'd be surprised how many 'green' and even experienced network marketers forget about or don't think about this crucial first step.

In order to have a recipe for success you're going to need certain resources, i.e. ingredients, regardless of anything else you may want to do—most of you will naturally want to put the horse before the cart—don't! You must have everything I'm going to layout for you in this chapter, before doing anything else. Again, if you do not get these ingredients, do not start cooking!

Why Ingredients?

Ingredients are important because if you were baking a cake and you started adding in random ingredients, chances are, by the time you finished baking that cake, assuming it wasn't already burnt to smithereens, because you didn't know exactly how long to cook it for or what temperature setting, chances are it wouldn't taste very good, and nobody, yourself included, would like it!

It is critical that you start any business with the right resources and tools at your disposal. Until you can afford the right tools for your trade, which I'll be outlining for you, I suggest you not embark in the trade. It would be like a bricklayer who didn't have a trowel, mortar, or bricks; it would be impossible to be a bricklayer. The same is true of the network marketer who didn't have his or her tools to network market; it would be impossible to be a network marketer.

Tools also make life easier. If people find a task too deterring due to the difficulty involved in carrying out the deed, the likelihood someone will begin but not finish is exponentially increased. Those are not probabilities you want; nor are they probabilities you want your team of new recruits enduring. This only creates a recipe for disaster and not success.

People typically in network marketing make decisions based on the risk/reward ratio. Let me give you an example: Say you happen to be talking to someone next week, after you've committed to joining a certain network marketing company, and you're talking with them and you tell the person you're trying to recruit, honestly, that most people in the company aren't making anything, but that the cost to get started is only $5,000. How many people do you honestly think will want to join your network marketing business opportunity? The reward is little, however the risk of losing $5000 is a likely reality for them should they join.

Now on the other hand, see a different example: Let's suppose you've joined a company and you're telling someone how you just got started yourself and you're already making $5000 per month in residual income, and that it only cost you $500 to get started. The reward potential in this example is greater than the risk/cost.

The point is you want to set people up for success in the beginning. If people are willing to commit to purchase what is necessary to do a job, then you can be assured that they are truly serious about the profession. A person who wants to be a carpenter, but who is not willing to invest in his carpenter's belt, framing hammer, or proper attire, isn't likely to last very long as a carpenter. The same can be said about the network marketer who isn't willing to invest in the right tools for the trade.

What Ingredients?

So what are the ingredients necessary for you to be a network marketer? If you ask a hundred network marketers you'll likely get a hundred different answers; most of these backed by some type of agenda, which usually includes making money off of you. I want to teach you, in my opinion, what you need, based on what I personally use. There is no personal agenda on my part. Chances are if you're reading this book you are not even in my network marketing business. If you are in my network marketing business chances are you've already purchased what I'm going to recommend already; elsewise you won't be in my organization—I wouldn't have allowed it!

The following resources I advise you to own:

I. **Laptop computer**: You'll want to own one that is up-to-date and which has a good processor, lots of storage capacity, a high definition webcam built in, and lots of RAM. Make sure it is USB 3.0/2.0 compatible, with a DVD burner.

II. **Wireless mouse**: Most laptops today come with a finger pad, which allows you to move your cursor. I advise you to get a wireless mouse (e.g., Gear Head, etc.) that allows you to more freedom in navigating. You'll thank your wrists once you do.

III.   **Wacom tablet**: There are many of these tablets to choose from and they range in price. The best one you can afford will do, but prefer you purchase an Intuos 4 or 5. You could purchase these on Amazon.com, last time I checked. These tablets will allow you to digitally write and draw using an accompanying writing instrument (e.g., Wacom pen) online. You'll be able to create lots of powerful content, which you will be doing a lot of, without having to blindly rely on others to do this for you; which can be pricey, to say the least.

IV.   **Adobe CC**: This is a paid subscription service purchased through www.adobe.com, which comes with a suite of software products you'll definitely want and need to learn to use. You can learn as you go—www.youtube.com is a great free starting place for learning almost anything. Included in this suite will be Photoshop, Premier Pro, After Effects, InDesign, Bridge, Audition, and many other software programs. These programs are a must have, in my opinion.

V.   **Microsoft Office 365**: This can be purchased through subscription as well through www.microsoft.com for about $100 per year for the 'Home edition'. If you already have Microsoft Word 2013, Excel 2013, and PowerPoint 2013, then you wouldn't need to purchase the subscription. Purchasing the subscription is a nice alternative as you'll get updates and the latest versions as they become available, without having to pay anymore.

VI. **H1 Zoom:** The H1 Zoom is a wireless hand recorder that (last time I checked) could be purchased on Amazon.com. The recorder allows you to record in MP3/Wav formats on a MicroSD chip that can be easily inserted into your computer for transferring the recorded files for uploading to the Internet. This recorder allows for up to 10 hours of non-stop recording before the batteries will need to be replaced. The cool thing is that the recorder will hold a 32 GB MicroSD chip, which will allow for more recording space than you'll ever need. Don't skimp and buy a less expensive recorder. I'm telling you this one has very clear recording, and makes life so much easier on you.

VII. **Sony EMC-CS3 lapel mic:** I like this particular lapel mic, because it can plug into my H1 Zoom and allow me to record with amazing clarity and sound quality into the H1 Zoom. The files once transferred sound amazing. This is invaluable to you when you create video training tutorials using Adobe Premier Pro editing software, because you can add in an audio track and edit it accordingly. Audio quality is important and shows professionalism. Don't skimp!

VIII. **Dragon Naturally Speaking Software**: This is the industry standard in "talk and type" software. Dragon allows you to speak into a microphone what it is you want to type and the words magically appear on your Microsoft Word document. Writing is as simple as speaking. This is important and will over the course of your business timeline save you a ton of time. Most people speak about 200 words per minute, whereas the fastest typists may find it challenging averaging 80 – 120 words per minute. Most people average typists can type between 30 and 60 words per minute—a far cry from 200 easily spoken words!

IX. **Express Scribe**: Express Scribe is an amazing, yet affordable, transcription software. I mentioned owning the H1 Zoom, well Express Scribe will allow you to take what you've recorded on the go, and quickly and efficiently transcribe it out into a Word document. What's nice about this software is the ability to slow-down or speed-up the audio recordings;

making it easier for you to keep up as you're typing what you've already recorded.

X. **Infinity Foot Pedal**: The Infinity food pedal is a USB foot pedal that sits beneath your desk. The foot pedal works with Express Scribe transcription software; making it so you can easily type while with your foot pausing and starting the audio. There's also fast-forward and rewind pedals in case you need to go back or forward on your audio recording, or if you simply need to find a particular place in the audio. Last time I checked both Express Scribe and the Infinity food pedal could be purchased on Amazon.com.

XI. **Headsets**: There are several brands and types of headsets you can purchase today. I recommend that you purchase and have three on you at all times. The first is a cheap, though amazingly great quality, Logitec headset that plugs into your audio and microphone jacks on your laptop. I paid about $15 for mine. The next is a Plantronics USB headset (e.g., Audio 478 USB Stereo Headset). I like this one in particular as it has a mute and volume button on the chord, i.e. making it easier to use. The last headset to purchase is a Logitec wireless USB headset. This is awesomely convenient to have when you're working with a potential business partner and you have to go to the bathroom or shut a door to your office to keep out the background interference. This being said, the charge on these do not last all day, and they do require charging.

XII.   **Lap desk**: A high quality lap desk can be purchased on Amazon.com. These allow you to position your laptop comfortably on your lap while you sit on your couch or in bed. They also can be used on your desk to help position your laptop in a more comfortable location.

XIII.   **Skype**: You'll want to download and create a Skype account. You'll also want to buy a Skype number which you can give out to potential customers and those in your down line so they can get in touch with you when needed. You'll also want to purchase a US/Canada annual calling plan. This allows you, for one low annual price, the ability to call any cell/landline phone through Skype. This can serve as your office phone; however, I would recommend you having a dedicated office phone that you can use. Usually you can get one for $10 through your local cable company.

XIV. **Smart Phone**: You'll want to own a recently updated smart phone that allows you to compute on the go and stay connected on the go. I do not recommend you giving everyone your cell phone number; instead, I recommend you downloading the Skype application on your smart phone and using it instead to make your prospecting/business calls. You need to be able to shut your business off when office hours are closed. If you want to stay married to your spouse; don't stay married to your business 24/7 365.

XV. **Digital Video Recorder**: You'll need a semi-professional/professional video recorder and a tri-pod. This will be used for shooting higher quality videos for trainings, etc. A webcam simply can't do what a high quality digital video recorder can.

XVI. **White/Blue/Green Screens**: You will need one white, blue, and green screen to use as back drops in your videos or when you're working in your home office communicating using Skype video. The white screen will be useful for when a light airy backdrop is needed. White backdrops are great for doing Apple-like presentation videos; like the ones Steve Jobs used to do in his black outfit, on white screen presenting. The green screen is useful for green screen productions using the Adobe Premier Pro Chroma-key function; allowing you to put yourself in different backdrop scenes (e.g., mansion, high-end hotel, conference room, etc.). The blue screen can be used either way; namely, to Chroma-key when you are wearing a green colored shirt, or to use as a professional neutral backdrop when you're wearing light colored clothes to give a contrast to you and your backdrop. These are an imperative—in no means will you ever be using the insides of your home/office as your backdrop. Image and your brand is everything and you must abide by this rule, always!

XVII.   **High Speed Internet**: You'll need a dedicated workspace (e.g., home office) that has high speed internet, i.e. wireless and hard line which plugs into your laptop.

XVIII.   **EazyPaper**: You will need a Microsoft Word plugin called EazyPaper (www.eazypaper.com) with 'Eazy X-ray'. This plugin will allow you to find synonyms for nearly every word you type and it will format all of your e-books and create an instant bibliography/reference page for you. I learned about this in college and have used in many times since graduating.

XIX.   **Books to own:** Besides this book I recommend you purchase all the other books from www.indirectknowledge.com as these deal with sales, marketing, infopreneurism, conversational hypnosis, question-based selling, and more. Also purchase all the flash card decks found on the website. Most, but not all, of these resources are available on Amazon.com, but you'll likely save money and waiting by purchasing directly from my website.

Chapter Summary & End Note Commentary

This chapter is all about the initial resources you'll need to be successful from the get-go in your network marketing business. So much of network marketing is producing information products regularly –and, these resources I've given you will help you do exactly this.

There will be a learning curve, but do not worry about that now. You'll be learning to master these software and technologies as you go. The longer you remain in the industry the more expert you'll become.

As a side note, you'll also need things I haven't mentioned on this laundry list of things to get; namely, anything you would need for a traditional office space. You'll need paperclips, stapler, notebooks, post-it notes, a filing cabinet or two, adequate lighting (e.g., desk lamp, etc.), bookshelves, comfortable office desk chair, microwave, mini-refrigerator, paper plates and plastic utensils, waste paper basket, etc.). Again, don't short-cut, and make sure you have all these things before you ever decide on what type of network marketing company to partner with, or before you do anything else.

The biggest mistake people make is getting started haphazardly. You want to ensure you're ready to truly pursue a career in network marketing, well before you ever commit to a company.

If achieving this first step is a hurdle you don't want to cross, then let me tell you upfront and honestly you will most likely not be successful in network marketing. If you're recruiting someone into your organization, and they are not able to fulfill these basic entry requirements, let me suggest that they aren't worth wasting your time with. Learn this lesson now and it will save you a ton of frustration, aggravation, and lost friendships later on. If people have any excuses as to why they cannot fulfill this basic requirement do yourself a favor and tell them until they are able to, you cannot work with them.

I cannot tell you in numbers how many people I have turned away from working with in my network marketing business who have given me excuses about acquiring these basic, yet essential, things.

Remember, when you do turn someone away use the recipe metaphor I've presented you with in this first chapter. There's never any need to hurt someone's feelings. Keep in mind, people who refuse who you turn away, will also respect you as a leader and often times reconnect with you after they realize how essential it is for them to own these tools.

I want you to learn one thing very well upfront here: recruiting people into your network marketing business is never about accepting everyone willing to join. You can, and most people do, recruit just anyone for a fast dollar or forty, but if people are noncompliant upfront, they will not succeed or help your business to grow, and, in fact, will actually, more often than not, impede your business growth.

It is imperative that you understand before you go into this whole new world of network marketing that not everybody is your market. I've had this discussion with thousands of people over the years. It's a hard lesson to learn, because people often think it is them that people are rejecting, when someone tells them 'no' and means it. This isn't at all the truth. The thing you must keep in mind is your target market.

Some time ago my nephew called me up out of the blue and was surprised to learn of a book I had written. He told me, "Uncle Bryan, I saw your book on Amazon, for like $29. Uncle B, I would have bought a copy, but I'm not going to spend $29 on a book Uncle B." Having been in Marketing and Sales most of my life, I knew straightaway what to say. I told him, "The reason you wouldn't spend $29 on a book of mine is because you're not my market. See, if you were my market you'd of whipped out your credit card without thinking twice about the price and purchased it right there and then and hoped it would turn up in the mail a day earlier than expected."

I share with you this story because it is precisely what we're talking about, and which you need to wrap your head around. When you are presenting an offer to your target market you'll seldom if ever have the headaches you'd have trying to sell a business opportunity to someone outside your market. This is not to say that people not in your target market won't buy or try their hand at network marketing, hoping it works out and makes their life better, it means that you'll almost always have better results when dealing directly with your target market.

Action Steps

The following action steps need to be completed before moving forward to the next chapter. These steps build and there is a purpose for having you do them—one that will be profitable in the end—so make sure you just do them without questioning or doubting my logic. I promise...everything will make sense soon enough. Trust the process.

I. Purchase all the ingredients (i.e., resources) I've mentioned in this first chapter. I want you to suspend your disbelief that I'm having you do this for the purpose of selling you more of my books and flashcards. I promise you they will help you and they are worth more than what they cost. This action step is not optional. You will want to do it, because it will help you acquire your end-goal sooner. Sooner or later you'll realize this and then you'll thank me you trusted me without question.

II.   Take your new H1 Zoom and record into it (without thinking too much about it) a 30 minute audio piece on why it's important to have these resources I've presented before you in this first chapter. Then using Express Scribe and your Infinity foot pedal transcribe the audio into a Microsoft Word document, and save it in a new folder labeled: "Network Marketing." Also include in this folder the audio you recorded.

III.   Take a full day to go through all of your new toys. Read one of the books. Open up one of the flashcard decks and rummage through the deck, studying the patterns. Just have a good day playing!

CHAPTER 2

Selecting a Company

J ust searching for network marketing on the Internet in a Google Search will land you tons of opportunities out there to choose from. There are literally thousands of companies that recruit thousands of network marketers every year. The question is: What's the best company to partner with?

Now you might be asking yourself why is picking the right company important to your success in network marketing? Well...

To answer this question we have to analyze ourselves inwardly. This means knowing what makes us tick. We have to understand our own persuasions and psychological makeup. You're not always going to understand why someone decides to go with a different company than go with your company. A lot has to do with the individual makeup of the person you're trying to recruit. What excites them may not be what excites you. Picking the right company is a big decision for anyone wanting to get involved in network marketing. It's not something to take lightly. You should not get excited about a company and just run with it without doing your own due diligence.

It's sort of comparable to someone wishing to get started for the first time in real estate. The person may be on their way to purchase their first property without having first analyzed and surveyed the market or investigating the property they're fixing to purchase. Picking the right property may land you an abundance of profit. However, picking the wrong property in the wrong location might end up being the worst financial decision you ever make—and the most costly!

The same can be said true of network marketing.

So how do you know what's the best company to choose? Much has to do with five criteria I recommend people use to initially assess and survey a company; namely: (a) what is the profit margin you can hope to achieve, (b) what is the name of the company, and is it attractive, (c) is the product one you can get behind and be excited about, (d) what are the costs (i.e., initial startup/buy in and ongoing monthly/annual fixed costs), and lastly (e) is this a company likely to be around a long time (i.e., how long has it been around and what might you assume about its particular industry in terms of the future)?

Sure there are other things to consider as well. These could be personal considerations about the company, products, or other people you may know involved with a certain company. These of course will be things you'll want and need to consider before a final decision can be made.

Why Do these Matter?

If you look at the profit margin and financial of the company by exploring the compensation plan and requirements for laddering up in the company some will certainly be more favorable than others. For this reason it is important to understand the compensation and to make comparisons of one in the industry you're most attracted to by comparing it with other plans in the same industry. If you're not likely to make the money you desire based on the compensation plan it really doesn't matter how great the company's product is or how emotionally attached you are to the said company. First and foremost you must consider the compensation plan and determine how feasible it is for you to earn a sizeable income or not. If you cannot make the numbers work in your favor I suggest you consider another company.

In Shakespear's play *Romeo & Juliet* Juliet tells Romeo, "What's in a name? That which we call a rose by any other name would smell as sweet." This might be true in the rational sense; however, we know the outcome of the play, and want not that for our network marketing business.

The truth is names are important. *A police officer* carries a different weight than *the sheriff*; yet, both are law enforcement offers sworn in to uphold the law of the land. Names carry meanings and sometimes strong meanings.

You'll quickly find in your investigating and due diligence of various companies some pretty outlandish nonsensical names tagged to many network marketing companies. A rule of thumb you might want to follow is whether or not you can pronounce and remember the name. If you cannot remember the name or feel an unpleasant queasy feeling in the pit of your stomach, others will too. Stay away from such companies. Make sure the company you decide to partner with has a neutral name or one that seems easy to remember and which seems to make good business sense. I also advise you to do an internet search by simply typing in the name of the company. Often times you can find the hidden meaning of a strange or unusual name by doing this. Some companies may have religious associations that would offend others outside that religion; making them and possibly you question the motivations and intentions of the company.

Different people have different tastes. What is attractive to you very well may be distasteful to someone else. You want to gain some feedback from other people about the products offered by a company you may be interested in pursuing. This feedback may be able to help you make a more informed decision and gain an objective non-biased opinion from others.

Additionally, you want to pick a product that has both practical value and intrinsic value. People make purchases based on the intrinsic or felt value they perceive about a product. This is because most people make a purchase based on the way they feel about the product even when they don't have any real knowledge of the product. This is why people will make a purchase without first experiencing a product when it is hyped up by professional sales copy the paces and leads the potential customer to feel a certain way about a product being promoted. You want to make sure the product you're backing has both types of value; both perceived and actual value.

Also it's worth taking mental stock in how one company's products vary from other competitors in the same industry—for example, if a customer buys weight loss pills from company 'A' and another customer purchases weight loss pills from company 'B' what is the difference. These differences are selling points. To know the difference all that is required is for you to look at the features or attributes of each product and do a side-by-side comparison of the two. This will give you immediate perspective about which company truly has a better product. It will also give you the answer to the question raised by a potential customer: "Why should I buy product 'A' instead of going with product 'B'?

Products also have features and benefits. The culmination of features and benefits fused with the right attributes the product possesses will give you a truly holistic perspective about the product you'll be marketing to your network and customer base. If you don't know your product it will be very challenging selling it to potential customers and business owners.

Considering costs is likely one of the first things a new business owner or potential customer will weigh side-by-side the product or company you're pitching to them. If the costs are not rational or logical immediately the sell could be a hard upward battle getting. For this reason you want to pick a company that has a fair pricing strategy.

A company that sets their prices too low will off-turn some buyers and business owners; rather than intrigue them into buying. Equally, a company who sets their prices well beyond the perception of the target market's intrinsic expectations will slow the growth of your business also.

The last thing you want to consider initially when surveying companies are the longevity of the company or how long has it been around. In network marketing it is trendy to jump on the latest greatest product launch and promote the heck out of it; however, you have to ask yourself: Is this a sustainable business model that I can and am willing to constantly support? For most people this would be an exhausting model to constantly be following.

On the flip side to this you have some companies who have been around so long that they've become boring or have eked out poor reputations. You don't want to involve yourself in a company with a bad reputation. In the Internet age most everyone will do a quick Google Search on a company to get some perspective and do their due diligence before making a commitment to join. I suggest, by the way, you do the same! Other people's feedback and painful experiences with a company will give you an idea of the type of company and their organizational culture to help you decide if it is one you can embrace or should stay as far away as possible from. Many people, and you are advised to also, check with the Better Business Bureau to find out if the company is in good standing or not. One that's not I advise you to stay away from, too.

What Will this Tell You?

Analyzing a company in this respect; that is, investigating the business model and compensation plan, learning about the name and its meaning, comparing products with other competing companies in the marketplace, factoring in costs and comparing these with practical and intrinsic value to determine how the market will likely respond to the offering being presented, and assessing the likelihood the company will be around for a long time or not, i.e. investigating the history of the company will all help you make a well-informed decision to partner and stand behind the company and their products or not.

Because there are so many companies to choose from in this day and age it is advantageous to skim the surface and survey these five critical points as opposed to going in depth with only a handful of companies.

The more companies you learn about through this survey approach will also help you in the future when someone thinking about joining your company brings to your attention your competition in the industry. If you've already surveyed a company already, which is a competing company, you'll have the answers already within you to be able to help win them over to your company. After all, it is wise and pragmatic to think that the same reasons you chose the company you did would likely be compelling enough an argument to help persuade your potential customer to come over to your way of thinking.

At the very least having a survey of the competition in your industry's marketplace will give you a broader perspective of what's all out there.

How Do We Take This Info and apply it to make the Right Decision?

I cannot over emphasize how critical this question is. I mean think about it: what persuades you to make a well-informed decision will in many cases be what persuades someone else to make the decision to join your new company or not.

What you want to consider first and foremost is how long it takes you to take action. The longer it takes you to join a company you can be assured others will take just as long. Keep in mind also that different people take longer or shorter to make decisions than others. Reflecting on your history of decision making will give you an intuitive sense of where you may mentally assess yourself on this scale. If you're a person who takes a longer period of time to make a decision to do something or not, then you may want to weigh this history into how long it's taking you now to make a decision to join a company or not. If you're taking longer than usual let this be a red 'warning' flag to you that tells you this company is a harder one to swallow for most people generally. The longer it takes you and others to join a network marketing company the less likely you are to succeed in promoting the company and its products.

A real problem is when you marry yourself to a company to the extent you exclude outright any other company. I've seen this phenomenon happen a lot with friends and former business partners of mine. They become engulfed in the thinking that they must join a certain company and not any other. Often when this phenomenon occurs the potential business partner outright rejects the possibility that some other opportunity may serve them better; largely they disregard learning about other opportunities and don't do hardly any due diligence. Please do not fall into this trap, or let your potential business partners fall into it either.

To be truly sold on your opportunity you must do your due diligence and take the road less traveled. It will make all the difference, because it will lessen for you and others the cognitive dissonance that occurs when you don't.

Cognitive dissonance is more or less 'buyer's remorse' and happens when you put the cart before the horse and don't consider objectively your decision to join a particular company; rather, instead you jump head first into the pool without checking to see if there's enough water to protect you from the fall. It is a mistake because after you've spent your money and committed it is often too late to go back, and you'll be like most people and wonder from time to time pensively: did I make the right decision?

Regret can happen and this sets you up mentally for failure before you've even had a chance to fully grow your business. The ugly cycle of quitting one business and starting another then occurs and you are always looking for the greener grass on the other side of a fence that does not exist. Your habit of joining one and then another and then another continues until you believe fully that the industry is flawed.

You cannot mistaken your abrupt starts and starts as indicative of how well the industry can take care of you or else you'll get a bad taste in your mouth for network marketing. The truth is network marketing is and should be run like any other type of business; that is to say, it takes time to grow a business, dedication to a system of operating it, and the ability to support it financially until it supports you financially.

I have a friend who started a restaurant five years ago with $190,000 it took him his whole life to save and putting in lots of long hours working for someone else. He didn't make a dime until his fourth year in business. Up until this point he was always paying himself back and putting profits back into maintaining operations of the business. Last year he earned a net profit of over $500,000. If you take $500,000 and divide it by five years you learn that he netted $100,000 per year, but it took him five years to get paid. The tortoise finished the race first; the rabbit went into the race with the wrong mindset and didn't win anything, rather took a loss.

This being said, most people when they join a network marketing business for the first time are extremely excited and full of big expectations and see an easy path to riches beyond their wildest dreams, quickly! If it were that easy to get wealthy in a network marketing company, especially stepping into it without knowing the ins and outs, then everyone would be doing it. Most people you know probably aren't! You'll know them because they are the ones ridiculing you for being involved in one.

If you treat your business like a hobby it will pay you like a hobby, i.e. you'll be giving your money away; on the other hand, if you treat it like a business it will pay you like a business. You have to understand the nature of business and how people get paid, and have the right expectations moving forward that it is not 'get rich quick' as the general rule of thumb.

How you make determinations about a company's name, compensation plan, longevity in the industry, products, and pricing structure is to study it and compare it right up side-by-side other compensation plans. It requires that you get out a calculator and calculate conservative estimates of return. You must also consider your mental makeup and determine if it is a company where you'd fit into the culture.

I was asked once to join a network marketing travel company by a truly great friend who is very successful in his company. I covered all the bases with and without him and it looked pretty good to me. I also had the inside scoop because he was my friend and I trusted him not to sell me but rather to do me a favor by helping me into the business. I never joined the business even though everything checked out legitimate and I could have made some great money had I joined. The reason? I never saw myself as a fun youthful individual who could enjoy myself at pep rally-like get-togethers. This was how the business functioned, and I didn't want to get that up close and personal with people and make it my entire life. I'm not comfortable with overly-extroverted activities. I'm a writer for goodness sakes!

My point for telling you this story is to have you really consider all the pros and cons, but also have you deeply and inwardly self-reflect on the type of person you are as an individual. Are you a social tycoon? Are you the lonely introvert? I want you to judge yourself honestly, because it will help you to make the right decision and to join the right company.

If You Follow this Advice?

If you heed the advice I'm advocating you'll be thankful in the end you did. Most everybody wants to make the right decision and it be a decision they want to make. The problem is you can want to join a particular company, but know it's not the right decision. You have to in these cases put away the heart and follow your head, honestly.

Do not sell yourself on an opportunity just because it is highly attractive and the sales pitch is world-class. If you do you'll get involved, spend your money, and go broke fast, before you ever make it over the learning curve.

You could, and I have, I must admit, join a company and spend thousands of dollars without making a penny and the company go belly-up without warning. Keep in mind that many network marketing companies are comparable to penny-stock companies that have little to no value. There are others of course that are worth millions of dollars and have been around for years and years.

If you were picking stocks to own for the long term you'd find those boring companies like Mars® and Procter & Gamble®. These companies offer solid returns over time. Alternatively if you wanted to invest in a hunch you had on a penny-stock found on some worthless pink-sheet you'd spend your money likely expecting to lose all you invested, not caring either way. We call this gambling. The house is operating a business; you're there to have a weekend of fun hitting buttons on a slot machine. I mean seriously who's going to come out on top more often than not financially, you or the house? You know the answer!

Analyzing a business requires critical thinking and the ability to set-aside your emotional nature and think with your common-sense 'reasoning' brain. Forecasting requires that you look at other peoples' success rates. This is usually found in the income disclosures companies put out about the profits being paid out. This can usually be found in the most obscure places on a website. Companies put them up to keep from getting harassed by the Federal Trade Commission (FTC). You can and should review them to learn for yourself how many people percentage-wise are making money, and then you can assume that everybody else is losing money. You'll see more often than not more people losing money and not making money.

Another trap people fall into is the false-illusion that they are somehow or in some way more equipped, more motivated, hungrier, and savvier than most everybody else out there who is losing money. If this is you, quit lying to yourself. The truth is there're people in this industry who've been around for years and years who have never made the money they first expected to make. If you ask these smart individuals how it is they're making the money they are today, which is still a fraction of their early expectations, they'll likely tell you it is because of consistently and over time working the system and growing their business.

So selecting the right company can be the difference between how long you remain in business or go back to working a 9 – 5. I encourage you to take your time with this early stage. It isn't glamorous doing all this research, but it can certainly be interesting to learn of all the different types of opportunities out there and how they compare next to their peers.

Chapter Summary & End Note Commentary

This chapter touched on some important points when selecting a company to partner with.

There are many companies you could choose, but choosing the right company is critical to your long term success. An easier way to select a company is by using the survey method: (a) deciphering the compensation plan of an individual company, (b) assessing its name and how people feel about it, (c) measuring the products by analyzing features, advantages, and benefits consumers will most likely gain in owning the product, (d) what are the costs you can expect to incur becoming involved with said company, and (e) how long has and likely will the company be around.

Taking this survey approach quickly gives you an idea about the value the company has and the goodwill it has amassed in the marketplace. Additionally though you'll want to, as you begin to narrow down the industry you want to operate within, and the various companies that appeal to you the most, you'll want to begin to learn about the company in far more greater detail. In other words, you'll want to check with the Better Business Bureau, as well do some in depth research on line to find out who the key players are in the company, what their reputations are, what the company's reputation is, talk to former business owners to learn their perspective on the company, and look for patterns that the company is either growing or contracting.

I once partnered with a network marketing company who only had one key player—an expert marketer and salesman. When he was offered ownership and other benefits by a competitor's company, in exchange for quitting the company I had partnered with, the company quickly went belly-up. I was out several thousand dollars by then; a costly mistake on my part for not doing my due diligence ahead of time.

Action Steps

I. Survey the network marketing industry as a whole and then, after you choose a particular subsection of the industry (e.g., personal development, health and beauty, wellness and nutrition, etc.) survey each of the companies that popup on a Google

Search (i.e., the major players) using the five survey criteria in this chapter.

II.   Use your H1 Zoom to record your thoughts about the pros and cons of each company. Take as long as you need into the recorder.

III.   Transfer the audio file into a Word document using Express Scribe and your Infinity foot pedal.

IV.   Select a company to partner with keeping in mind your own individual financial situation, long term costs you'll be incurring, upfront costs, products, company reputation, compensation plan, and the longevity of the company.

V.   Finish this phrase: "I selected this company because (a) ___, (b) ___, (c) ___, etc.

CHAPTER 3

Planning

As I recall, most people hate this chapter. Of all the chapters in this book this is the one least liked, but nearly the most important of all. If you find yourself hating this chapter I encourage you to keep in the back of your mind that it is likely to be the *only* chapter in this book you find yourself agitated with and wishing wasn't included.

> *"A goal without a plan is just a wish."*
> — *Antoine de Saint-Exupéry*

The reason I say this upfront is not to scare you or create a self-fulfilling prophecy that causes you to indirectly hate this chapter. The reason I say it is to prepare you in advance for the arduous journey ahead that is this chapter.

Benjamin Franklin coined the often used and now cliché quote: "By failing to prepare, you are preparing to fail." This instruction couldn't be any more true in network marketing.

When you recruit someone new into your business a large part of your obligation to the new business partner is to help them learn the system and plan out their new business.

The problem is most of the trainers aren't trained that well themselves, and so this makes it difficult to duplicate the training aspect of the system. Another big problem is when new people recruit new people and those new people they've recruited whom are usually friends and family do not observe them as strong leaders or even competent leaders in the industry.

If you were getting a job at McDonald's® do you think the management would have you being trained by someone else who just started a week earlier, or do you think they'd have you being trained by one of their senior employees? Unfortunately in the network marketing industry the new recruits are left often times to fend for themselves.

One of the reasons this happens is because the top leaders in the company, you know, the ones making all the money, don't have time to waste training newbies. Instead they'd prefer to spend their time upselling to their network their books or other products; claiming that these products will teach some great secret needed to be successful in the company.

These same leaders are the ones out on the beach, staying in posh hotels, and being praised as the top leaders by the owners of the company. All the time, they swear up and down that they are actively working their business as diligently as any new recruit would be.

Why is Planning Important

In network marketing, just like any business, especially a new one, planning is the critical factor for determining success. By now you own all the tools necessary for success that you picked up after venturing through chapter 1. You've selected a company you want to partner with, and paid your initial cost of ownership to get started with the company. Now you're left asking and unsurely wondering should I be doing what I been told to do by the person who recruited me? A feeling of doubtfulness is usually an indication you don't feel exactly sold on the person who sold you into the business opportunity. Maybe you see this person as being unsuccessful and therefore assume you must do something different in order to yourself be successful. A lot of thoughts are hitting you from all directions—trust me, I get it!

Planning ensures you know the facts about what you're facing and have a mental map about how to achieve your goals. Planning also gives you a solution or answer to achieving the end results you desire—for example, achieving an income level that allows you to work full time from home and be able to quit your job, without losing the income you need to pay your bills. Another example might be wanting to get to a point where you can live anywhere, around the world, without having to earn money in a foreign country or in a foreign currency.

Planning also gives you peace of mind knowing how much you're accomplishing as you work forward to complete your goals. Each step in the right direction is progress leading to the finish line you've been on the lookout for.

What Type of Planning?

The type of planning required all depends on the company you decide to partner with. Most companies these days have a laid out plan for you already. This is of course in their best interest and put before you with the intention of making them, i.e. the company, more money.

See most companies do market research on their products, business partners, and other areas of their business. They're expert at reading the data and making decisions that will increase the overall success of the parent company. After all they have many independent business owners, many of these IBOs are predestined for failure and factored into the success formula for the company. No. They will not share this fact with you. They probably assume you already know this if you've been in the network marketing industry for any length of time.

A big problem is when IBO's fall in love with the leaders of their companies. These leaders get raised onto pedestals as if they're some corporate god or something. When they speak people listen and respond accordingly. Mostly though it is the immediate person in your up-line who will connect with you and give you the attention you think you need. They're concern is keeping you as a business partner, because they're earning some type of income from the company having you as an IBO.

In fact, when you start calling them up on their personal cell phone whenever you like, and they take your call begrudgingly because they're afraid if they don't answer you'll slip off into your back office and ask for a refund or cancel your ownership in the company, costing them money, they call up with the cheeriest smile in their voice and treat you like the best friend they've always known.

What your immediate up-line doesn't understand is the value of their own time. I've seen it. I've been guilty of it myself, honestly. There's been many times throughout my network marketing timeline where I've been on the phone hours upon hours without ever getting paid for my advice, free resources, and time.

I mean keep in mind when you're on the phone trying to help someone struggling, often times lazy and wanting you to make the prospecting and sales calls for them, or wanting you to persuade them that success is just right around the corner, that you're not making your own sales calls, in effect losing income you could be gaining, losing out on opportunities. I found that a lot of the people I spent most of my time with on the phone were people honestly not capable or wanting to operate a network marketing company.

This brings me to another point: many people join a network marketing company for reasons other than working from home, making residual income, building a team of producing IBOs in their down-line, or for the reasons most might expect someone would want to join a network marketing business. These other reasons include simply the sales and marketing training provided by the company that can be repurposed over into their other sales job, to make new friends, to associate with people more successful than themselves, or even to pretend that they're more important and successful than they really are.

You have to watch out for these people. They will also hurt your desire to truly build a strong network of producers. When people are working for themselves from home, transitioning out of a 9 – 5 or some other just over broke J.O.B., they get anxiety, they get lonely, they get scared thinking they've just quit their job and now their income is dependent on their ability to sell other people into the same business opportunity that they've bought into. When people are afraid and terrified panicking having just thrown themselves into a disarray they don't think logically. This is also not the right mindset to be building a successful network marketing business. Your emotions will, whether you're aware of it or not, transfer like some contagious virus over into your organization. This virus-thinking as I like to call it, which others refer to as thinking negatively, is surely the fastest way to kill your down-line and have you down at the unemployment line, and hoping you can evade paying your rent without being tossed out on the street with no place to go.

For this reason I highly recommend that you as well as your down-line keep your day job and do your network marketing business part time until which time it replaces your income. This could be years by the way; rather than the months you might expect. For others it could be never!

Why do I mention all this doom and gloom and negativity? For one reason only: to help you protect yourself, value your time, and make sound business decisions that will grow and prosper your organization without hindering its growth potential. How do we achieve this? Proper planning is the answer!

So what type of planning is required? I mentioned earlier that your company will have some plans and systems already in place for you. Make sure you understand these plans and systems thoroughly, while also keeping in mind that your company realizes a lot of people will not make it in network marketing and so in their minds it is better to capture and gain as much as they can from you on the front end, because they suspect you won't last anyways.

The other types of planning I recommend is a solid professional business plan; not the one your company tells you to do, I'm referring to a business plan that has you consider every aspect of running your business. Another plan you will need to do, especially since you're in the marketing game now, is a marketing plan. Lastly I recommend you develop a Daily Method of Operations plan. This will be your daily instruction manual to help keep you on track and doing what makes you money and not what doesn't.

Before you make one sales call, tell one friend of family member about your new business, or listen to the person in your up-line telling you to make a list of 100 names and telephone numbers of friends, family members, and people you've had subtle contact with over the last ten years, stop, and do each one of these plans, first!

These plans will take time to do. In fact they will likely take longer than a week, working on them full time. Don't be dismayed, they will pay you back for the time spent in creating them possibly a million fold in the future.

I insist and require EVERYONE who joins my network marketing team to do one of each. I also insist that I must approve the plan before I'm willing to spend my precious time training someone to sell and market the products a company I partner with produces. If someone isn't willing to do these three things and do them well I don't want them as a business partner—plain and simple.

How to Write a Business, Marketing, and DMO plan?

Each one of these plans has a purpose. A business plan is in place to measure and monitor your business's growth and to provide a plan for how you will operate your business moving forward. A marketing plan is how you'll do your prospecting, advertising, promotions, and anything marketing related (e.g., product, price, promotion, placement). Anymore I require those that I work with to create a holistic marketing plan called an Integrated Marketing Communication's plan. This encompasses everything marketing related; from social media to guerilla marketing. Lastly, a daily method of operation is literally one of those day planners that marks out a space every 30 minutes from 12 am to 12 am the next morning, providing you a diary entry for what you should be doing during that specific time period. In business planning and making your plans actionable is critical for sustained growth. The longer you're in business the more money you should be making month to month. If you're not making more money at the end of year five than you were at the end of year four you need to revise your plan, because something is wrong.

Understand that plans must be measurable. You should be able to at some point spot-on forecast what you'll make at some future point. The power behind this is often not understood. Let me clarify: you want to be in a position to know probabilities and statistical inferences that you'll be able to achieve making 'x' amount of dollars in 'x' amount of months. Forecasting can be fun and even help to motivate you to achieve the results you are expecting or even to supersede them.

The Business Plan & Marketing Plan

A resource I learnt about in college which has helped me immensely with business plans and has furthered my learning about business is the website: www.score.org.

This website gives helpful advice about all sorts of issues businesses face from experts who've been there and done it—many time and time again.

For our purposes I want you to visit: http://www.score.org/resources/business-plan-template-startup-business

If this webpage is ever unavailable simply click on the search box found on the homepage of wwwscore.org and type in: business plan. This will get you to a template you can download and print off.

Anyway, once you're on this website I want you to click the download button and download the Microsoft Word business plan. You'll also note that inside the business plan is also a marketing plan. We're going to do both at the same time.

This document has instructions and step-by-step cookie cutter areas for you to fill in information as it pertains to your particular business. Remember, you're not doing a business plan for the company you're representing; rather, you're doing a business plan for your own independent business. So make it customized to you and your business ethics and person. Word it in such a way that will make sense to you; however, be pragmatic and professional. Keep in mind if you ever decide to take on a partner or apply for a business credit card you may likely be asked for a copy of your original business plan. So write it for you, but keep in mind you may have an audience analyzing it at some point in the future.

How to Write a DMO?

A daily method of operation or DMO is what you consistently do to generate results for your business; namely, it's a kind of journal you keep that allocates your time in terms of important activities day by day throughout your week.

Sure, everyone needs to make sales calls or else do prospecting for marketing campaigns, i.e. money producing activities, but people need to eat lunch, spend time with family, and take vacations from time to time. The point of the DMO is to ensure that you properly allocate your time wisely to where you're doing money producing activities consistently, while also helping you avoid situations like I mentioned before where a new business partner may try and eat up your time talking about how insecure they are, or to threaten you that they may need to opt out of the opportunity.

A DMO will also give you the ability to schedule appointments in 30 minute blocks of time. You never need to be on the phone with a new business partner for more than 30 minutes max. Most often a phone call should last fewer than 10 minutes and preferably less than five. You'll need to use your best judgment on this however. A DMO will also keep you from robbing yourself from spending too much time surfing the internet, needlessly, or doing things which aren't money producing activities.

To create a DMO all you need is either a digital or physical day planner that allows you to block your time in 30 minute intervals. Then what you do is create a block of time for various business activities. There should be so many hours set aside for prospecting new business, helping new business partners get the proper training (this book will help with that), and take deposits to the bank or do blogging for your branded website, etc. This DMO book will keep you on track day to day, and when asked by a spouse/partner what you did all day with your time you can pull out your DMO and tell them exactly.

What Will Happen if You Implement these Plans?

Implementing these plans will help you track success and measure your performance as a business owner. They are important because you'll be able to see your progress in a timeline format. You'll start to believe in your plan and sometimes discover ways to make your plan even better and more successful.

You'll also get a lot more accomplished in a much shorter period of time. The biggest problem I observe in this industry are too many people talking about doing something and not enough actually doing what they need to be doing. Usually this is a sign they're not cut-out for network marketing and should probably return to their day job making minimum wage. I'm not judging, but as you progress in this industry and grow your own business you'll see a lot of people fail, simply because they failed to plan accordingly to succeed.

Chapter Summary & End Note Summary

In this chapter you learned how to write a business plan, marketing plan, and put into action a daily method of operation (DMO). This chapter wasn't meant to intentionally fatigue your brain.

I purposefully made it as succinct and compact as possible to help you avoid feeling as if you have a lot of work to do. Really you do though; have a lot of work to do, that is. A business takes a lot of work if you want to be successful. You'll hear a lot of sales pitches from people who pretend to be successful business owners and from people who might have been born blessed into a wealthy family and so they're presenting their life as a result of their business acumen, when in fact it's because of their family wealth. Don't worry about other people and where they're at or what they have. Don't believe everything you hear or see.

Expert marketers can sell you a pretty picture and make their lifestyle seem like everything you've ever dreamt about; however, most of these marketers are blowing smoke and barely getting bad. They're intention is to promote their egos while trying to snatch onto your wallet.

A sound business requires proper planning. Any MBA will tell you this and if I were you I would value their opinion over an 18 year old kid who dropped out of high school. That's not to say that an 18 year old dropout can't own and operate a successful business over someone in their 40s; however, someone with proper education and knowhow I would value their opinion over someone trying to get my money at any cost who is promising me instant wealth systems and the code to unlocking the money tree—this is just hyperbole.

Action Steps

I.   Draft a formal business plan using the score.org business plan template I've given you the link to in this chapter. Take your time, cover every base, and really think through this thing fully. Also complete the marketing plan section.

II.   Decide on what format you want to record your Daily Method of Operation (DMO). Many tablets and smartphones come equipped with applications that are free or relatively inexpensive. Ensure that you have your day broken down hour by hour or by every half hour. Plan how many hours you will need to do money producing activities, personal activities, or routine necessary business activities. Plan your entire day setting aside time for family and miscellaneous activities. Never schedule miscellaneous appointments during the time you've set aside for working your business.

III.   Record an extensive audio track using you H1 Zoom, and then using Express Scribe and your Infinity pedal transcribe the audio fully into a MS Word document. Save both the audio and document into your 'Network Marketing' folder.

CHAPTER 4

Personal Branding

As a network marketer your brand is you from this point forward. Everything you put on the internet will never die from this point on, but it very well could kill your business if you're not fully conscious about what you post. I'm talking about branding you as an expert authority leader in this industry. Everything you do, say, and let or don't let happen, will, from this point forward, impact your business immeasurably.

Your brand is how you want to be represented to your publics. This is something you need to consider over and ponder in depth.

In this chapter I'm going to teach you how to brand yourself based on who you are as a human being. Branding is the difference between a generic product you buy at a local department and the name brand sitting right beside it. Branding is the goodwill a product has and the intrinsic value it possesses.

You can have two companies selling the same product with the same amount of debt, and the same actual value, and one can sell for million more than the other because it has goodwill and brand name recognition and the other does not. Really get the significance of this—it's important!

Why Brand Yourself?

People like people like themselves or people they look up to or respect or hold in high regard. The people most of us respect are strong leaders with strong values we can relate to. For many, our parents are the ones we respect the most and care the most about in our life. This is evident when a parent dies and is no longer in our life. The sadness and forlorn feelings we experience prove how valuable the parent was to the child.

Recently, some years ago, the company Hostess® was filing bankruptcy about to close their doors forever. The death of the company for Twinkie™ lovers brought with it the same pain that death brings with it when someone loses a loved one. I know, this is a peculiar phenomenon, but it happens none-the-less. It is the power of a brand and what that brand represents to consumers.

In the world of network marketing you'll find many people who have masterfully positioned themselves as top leaders of industry. Many people who have branded themselves as celebrity status authority figures have made not only a name for themselves but also created a powerful following of loyalists.

The primary benefit to branding yourself as a celebrity authority in your company is the money. Those who rank high in authority and expertise and who are the top performers happen-so because of the brand that they represent. For these powerful independent brands they could at any time leave one company and join another and most if not all of their down-line would follow them. For this reason they are extremely valuable to the companies they have partnered with. Companies will go to great lengths to help their brand and even pay their way to events and give them many other perks. This is much the same type of respect and consideration given a Hollywood movie star. They will be given free food just for associating themselves with another brand. If they were to visit a bar, for example, chances are the bar would pay for all their drinks, while worshiping them for making an appearance. Again, the power of branding!

What Does Branding Yourself Mean?

Branding yourself is creating an impactful way of presenting yourself onto others. Some people like to do this directly with in-your-face marketing. Others' preferences are to be more subtle; leaning on mystery and intrigue. Even others will start indirect and subtle and one they have the success behind them and the money begin marketing themselves much more directly and in-your-face.

When I think of branding I think of archetypes we discover in fictitious novels and Hollywood films. The characters are branded by the screenwriters and novelists to create a character you can empathize with and admire. People like underdogs who rise to the top of industry; that is, the classic rags to riches story. This type of archetype is one I especially relate well with and pattern myself after. Best of all it is not a lie I have to tell myself. I grew up in poverty and hand-me-down clothes and through this system of operating a business, i.e. the one I'm teaching you how to do now, I've risen to a high level of success and financial prosperity. Other archetypes are the rich kid who became richer. Or the Saint turned entrepreneur. Or the failure turned successful.

Speaking of the failure turned successful the first personality that comes to mind is Abraham Lincoln. He failed numerous times, time and time again, and eventually turn out to be President of the United States of America. He represents the epitome of personal branding success.

How to Brand Yourself?

I want to teach you branding the same way I was taught it. I want you to think of a ladder. We're going to start on the bottom of the ladder and work our way up. Then I'm going to give you some personal branding tips you might want to consider and use to brand yourself.

I.   Attributes: The first step to branding is determining what you represent in terms of attributes. This is exactly what brand managers and developers do when rolling out a new product. An attribute is something functional or unique about a product. I want you to transfer this over to you as a person and think about what makes you unique and how you function. When I was a kid my mother taught me that now to people are alike 100% just like no two snowflakes are the same either. Really assess yourself and discover what makes you truly you.

II. Advantages: Advantages are logical results which happen as a result of using or in our case with personal branding partnering with someone in business. Rationally speaking these are what the attributes you have will do for someone else when they decide to partner with you and join your network marketing business.

III. Benefits: Benefits are the emotional results that happen as a result of using or in our case with personal branding partnering with someone in business. Emotionally speaking these are what your uniquely valuable attributes and unique advantages will do for someone on an emotional level—for example, how will a new business partner feel after they come on board your team and partner with you?

IV. Values: When you consider a couple primary attributes, their logical advantages, and their emotional appeals, you can begin to holistically get a sense of what brand 'you' represents to the marketplace. You should be able in summary to simply state the essence or promise of your brand in a few words. After you are able to do this you begin to get a sense of the value you have to the marketplace and what that value represents to others, holistically speaking.

Congratulations—you're now branded!

Let's walk through an example though to give you a better understanding. Here's a table to make things easier to digest:

PERSONAL BRANDING LADDER	
VALUE➔	CARING
BENEFIT➔	ACCEPTANCE
ADVANTAGE➔	SOCIABLE
ATTRIBUTE➔	TALKS A LOT!

The above chart lists only one set of attributes, advantages, benefits, and values. I've done this intentionally so as not to confuse you; however, you will want to list probably three to five dominant attributes that are completely unique to your psychological profile or how you perceive yourself to be and how others likewise perceive you to be. The main thing with this exercise in branding is to be completely honest and forthcoming with yourself.

In the chart I thought about a friend I know and how I might would brand him. The first thing everybody always tells me after talking with him for the first time is that he talks a lot! This is a unique attribute you might say that defines him in a huge way. I then thought about how talking a lot might be advantageous to him and others. It occurred to me that people who talk a lot, at least the ones I've met anyway, tend to be social animals—true extroverts. Granted there are some negative pitfalls to being overly talkative, then again that's not the point right now. So the word 'sociable' came to mind. I can honestly say without thinking about it too deeply that my friend is truly sociable with other people. It's almost a natural extension of his personality. So how does this benefit him or the people he's sociable and talkative too? Benefits are the emotional response or emotional gain caused by a result of using or experiencing an attribute or advantage. It is also a critical thing to note that when people buy they usually make a buying decision based on their feeling and emotions and not so much on the logical advantages a particular feature performs. In the case of my friend the benefit to being sociable is his uncanny ability to make people (myself included) feel accepted and not judged. So I enjoy my friendship because I know my friend accepts me and I have to assume just about everyone else he interacts with.

So what's the essence of all this? I mean when you think about my friend, never having met him before, just knowing that he's talkative, sociable with others, and leaves people feeling accepted, what would you conclude is the essence of his personality? You guessed it, or else looked at the chart, it's the value he hold for others, which is he's caring.

If my friend were prospecting someone into a network marketing business do you think they would be more attracted to joining a business with someone who truly cares about them and wants to help them, or someone who is a shell of a personality who hides behind a mask and who is unapproachable? It's obvious, isn't it?

My friend, would want to use this innate brand promise to strongly promote himself as this wonderfully caring humanistic representation of all that is good and kindhearted in the world. He would want to associate himself and his brand image with similar associations people make when thinking of an altruistic personality who cares about everybody equally.

So you get the idea of how a brand is developed by discovering the innate promise a produce, or in this case an individual possesses, and then promoting according and in alignment with that very precise promise.

I want to share with you another point which leads back to a point I was making moments earlier. When you discover your unique brand and can state it in a few words, like a unique slogan, be aware that there are pros and cons of anything positive. We see this happen with political figures. The candidate's party will emphasize the brand promise by relating everything the candidate has ever done or said back to the persona of the candidate. On the flipside the opponents will take this brand and contrast why it is detrimental to the position the candidate is running for. In just about everything good and favorable there's a flipside that's ugly and unfavorable. The opponents to the party and the candidate will use polarity branding to paint a different picture of the candidate that runs contrary to what the candidate's party is trying to emphasize. May the best party win—or lose!

Keep this polarity in mind when you are branding yourself because you want to expect that what you think is positive and noble will for some people be a negative in their mindsets.

Personal Branding Tips

The following are some tips to keep in mind when you are branding yourself to others:

I. You are your brand: This means everything you do from this point forward must be in alignment and completely congruent with the brand you're representing—for example, how you treat others, how you answer an email, how you sell, how you communicate, etc.

II. Everything you do or don't do will impact your brand: This means making it an imperative to stay true to your brand by making decisions that will advance your brand and how you want other people to perceive you as. It doesn't mean making a rash decision just because it will impact you in the short run financially, or make you become perceived as more powerful. You must refrain from being incongruent with your brand at all costs.

III. Everything online lives forever: This means you must consider every action you make. Understand that people respond differently based on how they feel. Do not let your emotions make you post an incongruent Facebook post, just because you're feeling excited about a new sale you've just made, or because you're upset about a relationship gone wrong. Never be reactive in your communications; rather, instead, wait until your frame of mind allows you to make logical decisions.

IV. Proofread everything: This means making completely sure your grammar and spelling is always correct. There's no excuse for this when MS Word offers spellchecking. Don't rely on using WordPad/Notepad as there's often times no spellchecker working to ensure your spelling is correct. People with poor spelling are instantly branded as incompetent and a turnoff for many people to want to work with.

V.   Always be giving value: This means making it a point to share an aspect of yourself worth with others. This could mean sharing a story or giving away something for free. This will also help people perceive you generous and their reciprocity will likely be of tremendous value later on to you. When you do give away something of value make sure you get the credit for it.

VI.   Be on time: This means never being unpredictable. It means when you tell someone you'll call them at 12:20 in the afternoon that you call them exactly at 12:20 in the afternoon. This will ensure other people value your time, but it will also create trust and confidence in you, and position you as a true leader they can rely on.

VII.   Never brandish success; reflect on it instead: This means being modest and instead of flaunting your success or throwing your success in someone else's face, instead talk about the journey it took you to become successful. This is a much more powerful way to exhibit that you are successful—an indirect approach.

VIII.   Perpetually hold integrity for your brand: This means never ever doing anything to compromise your brand promise and what you represent to others. It means never acting one way around some people and another way around others. You must remain honest in your brand and the rest of the pieces I've mentioned will stick together. Integrity is the glue that holds these parts together. Never let anyone question your integrity and truth—your brand will fall apart if you do. Your character and the vows you make to uphold your value is all you have. Master this and you'll succeed where many have failed and quickly rise to the top of your company.

Chapter Summary & End Note Commentary

In this chapter you learned all about the importance of branding and personal branding and how to create a brand and even some powerful tips to maintain your brand and rise to the top of your company.

It is important at this phase of your new business to create a brand strategy that delivers on the promise of the image you wish to represent to others. People don't like wishy-washy unpredictable people. They like people who are readable and easy to make sense and relate with.

As you grow your business never forget your brand. The brand is your roots. Many people get off-put when someone they knew as poor comes into an inheritance of great wealth and the person changes to reflect something they no longer wish to identify with. Your brand is what will take you to the top; however, if you lose your brand when you reach their, chances are you'll not be their long. So staying congruent in how your represent yourself, your personality, your style, your communication standards, and so on, is vital to your continued success.

I knew a guy once, a network marketer, who was the nicest more genuine and authentic person you ever met in your life, and he became quite successful in his industry. The wealthier he became the more he changed; to the extent I couldn't stand being around him anymore. Today the guy is no longer in the industry and he is not wealthy; however, he's become much more humble and kind to others and not so egocentric.

When I think of someone who holds true to their brand I think of Oprah. She came from poor roots, but her personality has not changed. She maintains the integrity of her brand beyond anyone I've ever studied. Regardless of how poor someone might be they would still feel comfortable and welcome in her presence—she's authentic—she's also a billionaire. Food for thought!

Action Steps

I. Find your brand by utilizing the laddering approach I've revealed to you in this chapter. Understand your brand promise and in three or four words write a slogan that represents the essence of your unique brand.

II.   Create a brand strategy in which you will make yourself and all your actions reflect congruently this brand.

III.   Write on a 3x5 index card your brand promise and hang it over your desk where you will see it every day while working your business. Let it be a constant reminder of what you represent to others. Never take any action, whether for quick self-gain or an increase in power, if it contradicts your brand.

IV.   Never sacrifice your brand image to make a sale. If you do you will lose your most valuable asset and all the goodwill you've built into your brand.

V.   Record into your H1 Zoom the process you took to develop your brand. Talk about any hiccups you experienced and talk about the importance of branding yourself in this way and what you expect your brand to do for you in terms of increasing your personal value to others. Then transfer it into a Word document and save both the audio and the Word document in your 'Network Marketing' folder.

CHAPTER 5

Marketing MBA Style

Marketing is the heart of what we do as a network marketer. We market our company's products, the parent company, our company, and ourselves. At first it may seem like a daunting task. The reason for this is because everyone starting out, okay well most everyone, thinks they have to do everything all at once, in order to make money.

At this point I want to reemphasize that the longer you're in this profession, this industry if you will, the more money you will make. It doesn't happen overnight. You can, however, make money overnight. What I mean is you can make 'some' money, but after some time you'll make even more money. This is because you will not only learn how to make more money, but your opportunities to make more money will increase as you build your business. Network marketing businesses have a compounding or multiplying effect. You recruit one person you make money. They recruit someone you've made more money with less effort if any extra effort. You stop recruiting, and they continue recruiting, you still make money, but not as much as you would if you were still recruiting others yourself. It is important to stay in the game because in the game is where the money is.

I'm going to teach you a new approach to marketing. This approach is what you would learn if you were sitting in an MBA program at some expensive private university. Don't worry though, because I'm not going to charge you the quarter million dollars it cost me to learn this knowledge. I appreciate you simply buying my book. Incidentally, how's that for value?

This modern approach is an integrated marketing communications and advertising approach. Companies pay MBA's big money to integrate their communication channels, making this a holistic approach.

Why Should You Learn This Approach?

This approach to marketing is going to give you the upper hand on most all other network marketers. Since you're in network marketing I'm sure by the end of this chapter you'll appreciate what you've gained from this lesson.

You will also be learning about your target market. I have a unique way to help you determine your target market, which I'll be sharing with you.

The integrated approach also happens to be a holistic approach; it examines every element of a business to connect completely through every channel the marketing message. We start with consumers, then look at competitors, and finally, the last 'c' communications. All of these three c's are vital to marketing in the most effective way possible.

What is Integrated Marketing Communications?

Besides just being a holistic approach to conveying a marketing message throughout all communication channels present in a company; an IMC also takes into consideration other non-traditional marketing outlets and pulls all these external opportunities to convey a message together into one centralized plan. All the parts work together to ensure the greatest advertising and marketing impact, and everything gets measured and analyzed continually on an ongoing basis.

As a network marketer you are a brand ambassador for the company you've chosen to represent and partner with. It is your primary job to promote products and the business opportunity. The parent company exponentially grows when all the agents in the organization are continually recruiting. They embrace this because it saves them millions, possibly billions, of dollars each year on advertising and promoting their products.

From this point on though I want you to imagine that you own the company and you're the only person promoting the products you're offering. Take ownership in your mind for the time being, because I want to help develop an IMC plan that will ensure you market effectively.

We're going to learn about the target market. Most network marketers get this wrong. Most don't probably know what a target market is, I might assume from my experiences working with enough of them. The customer leads us into exploring what makes our customer tick; that is, consumer behavior and buying psychology. The next element we'll address is our competition. You want your marketing to pull in more and more market share, i.e. you want a bigger piece of the total market. The more market share you pull in the more money you'll be making and even more than that the more the multiplier effect will work in your favor to quickly dominate the market. The last element you'll be learning has to do with communications.

I know you're probably excited to get started, aren't you!? Okay, let's do it!

How to Create an IMC Plan?

In this section I'm going to teach you step by step how to design your own IMC plan. We'll take this a subsection at a time and cover the each of the three c's. After this we'll pull everything together and I'll teach you how to measure the effectiveness of your marketing efforts in a flawlessly easy way.

As a side note: this chapter will likely stretch a bit longer than most of the others, but this is network *marketing*, is it not? This chapter contains the essential nuts-and-bolts of what we do in this industry.

Marketing can be a lot of fun, and in fact, you do use a lot of creativity in promoting your offerings. You also get to exercise your brain more cognitively as well as you process steps, and analyze information.

Customer Component

I mentioned earlier that I was going to give you a tip on how to quickly find your target market. I'll do this now. Because you're a new business owner promoting an already established entity, i.e. the parent company, it is easy to find out your target market, because all you have to do is survey the existing customer base and other independent business owners. Ask yourself what do they all have in common? Do they make up one primary demographic; that is, are they mostly men, mostly young men, mostly young vegetarian men, mostly young vegetarian men concerned about the environment? What you want to do is narrow down as precisely as possible the overall market. The narrower your focus the better you'll understand the people you'll be marketing to. The better you understand this the better you can focus your marketing resources to gain the best results.

I've asked a lot of new network marketers this question: Who are you marketing to? The answer I get most of the time is: Everyone!

This could not be further from the truth. You are never marketing to everyone unless you happen to be Coca-Cola® or Pepsi® attracting a mass market of sugary beverage drinkers. It costs those companies billions every year in advertising dollars. Most internet marketers I know don't have billions to spend on marketing, I suspect you don't either. So we want to find our best customer. You know, the person when we ring em' up and ask them if they want to buy product 'x' instantly gets excited and can't wait to give you their credit card number.

In an IMC you want to study current customers, former customers, potential new customers, as well as your competitors' customers. The easiest, as I've just revealed to you, is the current customers.

Former customers will take time, as you probably don't have anyone who has dropped out of your organization yet, assuming you haven't actually begun any type of marketing yet. When you do experience some of your network dropping out you'll want to analyze why. Their feedback when you have that last conversation with them may not reveal everything honestly, but keep trying, because the more you learn from their feedback the better you can ensure that you don't make the same mistakes again. Potential new customers will be other people in your target market. You'll want to learn as much as you can about your target market because this will help you communicate with them in language they can understand in effectively sell them your business opportunity and products. The last group are your competitors' customers. These are people who opted to join them instead of you. You want to find out why! Then you want to determine how you can sway them away from the company they picked and persuade them to come over to your company and join your team.

Realize competition is good because it keeps companies legitimate, keeps pricing affordable, and creates a culture of constant improvement and innovation happening which customers get excited about and want to buy into.

Competitor Component

Your competitors are always trying to outflank you and capture your share of the market extending their reach and profits. We can't point the no-no finger at them though because we're constantly doing the same thing ourselves—why they call it competition!

One superb way to know the cutting edge marketing approaches and outlets through which you can connect your marketing message with consumers is by studying what your competition is doing. Then steal their approach and make it your own. Easy enough, eh?

You must identify all of your competitors and keep a constant eye on them and what they're doing to attract and retain customers. Corporate espionage? Absolutely!

This means studying their websites, subscribing to their email lists, going in search for their promotional materials, even looking at their annual reports if you can gain access to them. Note: Publicly traded companies are required to make this information public. You can find it doing a simple Google Search.

Once you find out who their customers are and get to know them and distinguish why they chose them over you, then you can start zeroing in on the most effective ways to steal them away from your competition. You'll want to certainly identify the strengths of your competition, their weaknesses, where they may have opportunities, but also what might pose a threat to their organization. Wouldn't it be great if your company were their greatest threat? I bet it would be!

In business we would call this doing a simple S.W.O.T. analysis. You can Google Search or YouTube how to do one. I assure you they're easy to master.

Communication Component

Communication at first seems like an easy thing to do for most people. You simply advertise, someone sees your ad, they call, you sell them your product and opportunity, and you hang-up the phone, and wait for it to ring again. It's not that easy anymore.

Everyday people are bombarded with advertisement after advertisement. In the world of advertising they have two terms you should know as a network marketer; namely: (a) Clutter, i.e. the quantity of marketing messages being pushed onto consumers due to the ever increasing competition and need for companies to attract these customers, and (b) Noise, i.e. an ineffective marketing message that presents an advert that is distracting or confusion in which the market doesn't realize what's actually being promoted.

To keep clutter from happening more and more marketers are utilizing alternative marketing methods like: guerilla marketing tactics, viral marketing, and experiential marketing. You can likewise learn about these by doing a simply Google Search.

To eliminate the problem of noise marketers are more and more frequently employing test groups to determine if a message sticks or gets filtered out. Again, this highlights the importance of always gaining feedback from everyone you speak with. I've gotten a lot of my best marketing ideas from other people's feedback. I encourage you to do the same. The best way, in my opinion, to learn about your market is to talk directly to them in a way that is neutral and curious. You don't want them to think the only reason you're asking for their feedback is to sell them something more.

So we discussed target marketing. This is learning the demographics of your best market, also what they like to do, who they are, how do they think, what's their level of education, their income levels, their average age?

You also want to consider psychographic information. This is information that has to do with your target market's activities, interests, and opinions. Take in that these alone will not tell you the likelihood someone will or won't buy your product or opportunity. They are just a frame of reference to help you get into the heads of your target market.

A great resource I'll share with you is the VALS psychographic segmentation framework. You can learn about the different types of psychographic demographic by visiting this website:

http://www.strategicbusinessinsights.com/vals/ustypes.shtml

Traditional media channels included: (a) television, (b) radio, (c) outdoor, and (d) magazines, and (e) newspaper advertising. These at one time in history consumed nearly 100% of all advertisements globally. Today this is not the case anymore. New media outlets have created new opportunities for advertisers and marketers to get their marketing communication messages out to consumers. One of these is e-active marketing. E-active marketing utilizes two components of internet marketing; namely, e-commerce and interactive marketing.

E-commerce has many subcomponents: (a) online catalogs, (b) shopping carts, (c) payment methods, (d) store locators, (e) customization of products to suite particular customer needs and desires, and (f) customer reviews and feedback.

There are a lot of incentives to owning and operating online as opposed to owning and operating a traditional brick-and-mortar business with four walls and a ceiling. These include: (a) increased reach opportunities, (b) reduced shipping costs because they're passed along to buyers, (c) fewer labor costs, (d) lower personnel costs (e.g., outsourced digital labor), (e) operate 24/7 365, and (f) the ability to pass along savings to consumers. Measuring customer behavior patterns is also something that has become prominent in today's e-commerce world. When customers make purchases they are recorded and ad-specific promotions can be customized and passed straight to them via email or online display ads.

Interactive marketing is much as you might expect by the name. It creates an interactive interplay between the potential customer and the company. In this approach the customer is no longer left to remain in a passive marketing role, but rather encouraged and persuaded to be an active participant in the interchange of product purchases. Some of these tactics marketers utilize frequently which I would encourage you to become acquainted with are: (a) banner ads, (b) blogs, (c) email marketing, (d) email newsletters, (e) online promotions, (f) podcasts, (g) social networks, (h) search engines, and (i) viral campaigns.

Online advertising takes on many outlets. There are display ads that can be purchased which show up when a consumer has investigated purchasing something and a cookie shows up on their browser to record activity and then display the appropriately targeted ads in which consumers are most likely to be interested in. This, by the way, is a great means of targeting a specifically interested consumer. There's also pay-per-click ads sold through search engine providers as well as some social media outlets.

There're also many ways people are using some micro—blogging platforms for relaying promotional messages, or to serve as customer service vehicles that are manned 24/7 by companies. Many companies have gotten extremely creative in how they adapt new web 2.0 technologies to meet the needs of customers and the company, while also targeting their competitions' customers.

With e-active marketing also comes direct response marketing, which as a network marketer you will want to learn as much about as possible. These include email, web analytics to direct email, email newsletters, and viral marketing.

Assuming you're new to network marketing you should be alerted that you should subscribe to an email autoresponder service. This is a company which allows you to store in a database a list of email addresses and names, but also which lets you create emails in advance and send them out automatically over a set interval of time. There are many companies you might want to explore subscribing to. To get started I would recommend you check out MailChimp.com, Aweber.com, GetResponse.com, and ConstantContact.com. These are some of the most well known in the industry and all of these companies have comparable rates.

As you collect lead information from potential customers you'll want to add these emails and names to your database through a double-opt-in-form (also provided by the email autoresponder company). Whenever someone visits your website they will be encourages through some type of free offer you use to attract them to fill in their name and email which will automatically subscribe them to your list.

I mentioned viral marketing and want to further clarify what is meant by viral marketing. Viral marketing is a means by which a marketing message is passed from one person online to another person online and can take the form of a YouTube.com video, email, a blog post, or even a social media post that gets passed around. This form of advertising makes it easy and inexpensive to reach a large number of people online in a relatively short period of time.

Now, the next type of marketing communications is known as alternative marketing. This marketing consists of several components: (a) buzz marketing, (b) guerilla marketing, (c) lifestyle marketing, (d) experiential marketing, and lastly (e) product placement and branded entertainment. I'll cover each of these briefly as well and let you do more research on them by doing a simple Google Search.

I. Buzz Marketing: This is essentially word-of-mouth advertising in which buyers pass along information about products to other potential customers. You'll personally be doing a lot of this buzz marketing as a network marketer. In fact, some network marketing companies do this form of advertising and marketing through hosting house parties. Keep in mind that some conditions make the buzz more enticing and encourages greater reach for the word-of-mouth. These include: unique product features consumers can get excited about, the outlet for marketing in this fashion should be memorable, people should be intrigued, and often times it needs to be a product that is different, i.e. outside the mainstream. A special form of buzz marketing is called Stealth Marketing. This is something you want to take note of as a network marketer, because stealth marketing is when a marketer, posing as a consumer, introduces a product indirectly to another consumer, selling up the product and how much they like it—never revealing their motivations for doing so. Social media is also a great place for hyping up products, as well as forums, where you might hide your true identity by adopting a pseudonym and after posting some benignly helpful posts make a recommendation to others where they might be directed to your network marketing website or your blog. Many top internet marketers recommend this approach and have revealed openly how it has helped them grow their customer base.

II. Guerilla Marketing: These marketing tactics rely on heavy creativity, and originality. If done right though, they create a lot of attention and as you might guess a lot of goodwill and praise, but also sales, for the company. As a new network marketer you'll likely start with a small advertising and marketing budget to get you started, and guerilla marketing is a relatively inexpensive tactic to add to your IMC mix. To get an idea of how Coca Cola has successfully implemented this into their mix watch this video:

https://www.youtube.com/watch?v=lqT_d PApj9U. As of the publication of this book the company received over six million views to this video. It cost Coke very little to make this video, but as you might imagine it has paid off in huge dividends while also supporting Coke's brand promise. Who wouldn't be happy with Coke after watching this video?

III. Lifestyle Marketing: This is another option for you as a network marketer. Lifestyle marketing is plain and simply when you associate your product with a particular consumer interest group (e.g., hobbyist group, entertainment venues, etc.). For example if you're promoting a company and a product that is in the nutrition industry, you may want to see about joining a www.meetup.com group that has some association with nutrition. Then you can directly sponsor or promote your product and business opportunity to the group when appropriate. I knew a network marketer who had real success sponsoring a business luncheon once a month where business professionals could get together and network with one another. Every time she hosted the event she required a $10 dollar donation which paid for the meal, but also helped pay for her efforts in hosting the luncheon. She also used it as an opportunity to share a business opportunity DVD with the group while also taking it as an opportunity to get business cards from everyone present which she added to your email list.

IV.   Experiential Marketing: This is a newer form of alternative marketing which has recently hit the scene. It involves a combination of direct marketing, field marketing, and sales promotions. An example is when I recently went to enter a local department store to purchase a few items and discovered just outside the doors a funny looking clown truck that was specifically designed to introduce me and others entering the store a particular line of smartphones. I was given a free gift after I was given the opportunity to throw a ball at a funny looking target. I was also given a steep coupon discount in exchange for making an immediate commitment to purchase a new phone right then. I didn't buy, but I can't get the experience out of my head either, and I remember telling several friends and a couple family members about my experience. It was fun!

V.   Product Placement: This is also another interesting means of alternative marketing. It is when marketers arrange to have their products and brands show up in movies, and other outlets that cause people to experience different emotions. Since people tend to be in the mood to buy when they are excited, it could be that a company strategically places a product in front of a customer through an indirect means right immediately before the climax. As a network marketer you may not utilize this approach in the most traditional sense, but you could, I suppose, create your own mini-movies and host them freely on YouTube.com or Vimeo.com, and do essentially the same thing, only have your call to action in the comments fields or even at the end of the mini-clip.

VI.   Cinema Advertising: This is the last one I'll cover, but one I experienced tonight while at the movies. It is the ads placed on the projector screen just prior to a movie. Depending on your location and your local theatre's requirements you may possibly find this a great outlet to reach some local customers. Of course you could call up a theatre in a larger location and advertise there as well.

I've given you quite a bit to consider, and I didn't even mention one of my favorites and a great one for network marketers, and that's sweepstakes. You can create a sweepstakes campaign by visiting sites like: www.sweepsadvantage.com. The cost is miniscule, but you'll still want to measure this outlet just like any other in your IMC mix.

Now that you've got all these great ideas it's time to formulate a strategy. How you go about this is to consider your budget, talents, and resources and find the best way to reach the most amount of potential customers specifically marketing to your target market. This will take some discovery and time, but you definitely want to do it, and do it right. So start by allocating a little money to those communication outlets that intrigue you the most. Also you want to perhaps target some of your competitions' customers using some of these outlets by putting forth targeted messages that will persuade them to come over and dip their toe in your pond.

Lastly you want to measure your campaigns to determine how well each is converting traffic into sales. A little secret for monitoring all of this in one single location is to have a WordPress website/blog setup in which you first direct all you traffic there. Using a plugin like JetPack will allow you to track all of your incoming traffic and measure and store the data for you at no cost. I find this to be an inexpensive way of measuring my marketing campaigns and I can see on a graph which methods are working best for me. Off line campaigns will have to be measured too but you can do that in a number of ways too. One way is to use a toll free phone number and attach it to your advertising. Have a different number for each outside outlet. When a potential customer calls the number there will be a record of it and you'll be able to know and track it to determine how effective the ad is.

Setting-up a Website?

I would find it nearly impossible to be a network marketer without having my own personally branded website. I'm not talking about those identical but personally branded copy-cat sites your network marketing gives you. You do not want to direct traffic there until it is time to sign up your new business associate.

Instead you want to have a blog or website that allows you to interact, entertain, sell other products from, and collect customer contact information.

The easiest way I find to do this and most professional is to set up a self-hosted WordPress blog. Don't be confused thinking I mean a free WordPress.com blog, because I'm talking about one you setup and host yourself independently, the WordPress.org type.

What I do is first visit either Bluehost.com or Hostgator.com and setup a hosting account. This can be done for between 4 – 10 dollars a month. Usually this includes or allows you to also setup a domain name. This is the name people will type into their web browser to be taken to your blog/website.

I suggest you pick a name that is easy to remember, not off-putting, and as professional as you can. The shorter the better, and keep in mind your personal branding. It must be congruent with your personal brand.

After you've gotten your domain and your user name and password to sign into your c-panel account there will be several options, one of which is a WordPress blog. Choose this one and continue following along until you have the theme and dashboard activated. Once your blog is up and going you can start creating useful content to start adding that will bring value to others who stumble upon it, but which also represents your personal brand.

Depending on what you want to do with this site will depend on the types of free plugins you decide to use. Like I mentioned earlier the JetPack plugin is a wonderful one for measuring your IMC plan.

For more on how to setup a WordPress website I suggest you visit YouTube and search for a few tutorial videos. There are several which are real informative which will get you up and going quickly.

The purpose of having your own website are manyfold. For one it gives you an outlet to provide content to others over the internet. It also provides a vehicle to let you sell other e-commerce products and information products. Refer to my book "The Infopreneur" to learn more about how to create these types of products quickly and easily. Having your own blog also can serve as a means to integrate many if not all of your integrated marketing communication outlets. For example, I use mine to blog, post contests, I have all my social media integrated when when I post a blog post, it also automatically posts to Facebook and Twitter and other outlets. I also have

YouTube videos which I embed into blog posts that link back to my YouTube.com account. So you see how necessary your own website is if you are an internet marketer.

The last thing I want to say about having your own blog is that it allows you to communicate with your network marketing team without having to stay connected via phone. My team are actually subscribed to www.indirectknowledge.com so whenever I post something they receive an immediate email from me with the new blog post. They can then share the content with friends, family members, or others further down the down-line.

What if You Decide to Do Something Different?

This is absolutely fine. Honestly, I encourage you to play around and figure out the best IMC marketing strategy that works for your particular industry and what you've got going on.

Your marketing budget will also dictate what you decide to do to generate traffic. You may want to start small, while you're still employed, until which time you've recruited a handful of new IBOs until you start to get more diversified with your marketing promotional mix.

I know many, and I have to admit I'm in this group also, network marketers who make marketing a fun game. Getting your marketing perfect or right seldom happens if ever. You're always tweaking it and trying something new. When you find something that is converting real well it will likely be something you'll want to allocate a larger portion of your budget towards. Alternatively when you discover an outlet converting extremely poorly it may be something you will want to opt-out of altogether or test it using a different bit of sales copy.

The whole point is to just have fun and gain some green in the process.

Chapter Summary & End Note Commentary

In this chapter you learned about the three c's of the integrated marketing communications plan. You've also learned about many varied forms of advertising and promotion. You've also learned how to measure and track conversions. I've even taught you very generally how to setup a weblog style website that can be used to bring all the various components of your marketing communications together so they can be measured and statistics performed.

Even though I may be quite general at times in explaining what I've brought in front of you, I've done so for the purpose of presenting you with a lot of information that can be instantly researched online in a matter of minutes which will give you better instructions and perspective.

The reason behind this is I could write an entire 500 page volume on just one aspect of marketing (e.g., social media). I don't want the purpose of this book to bog you down making your forget or get overwhelmed by everything I'm throwing at you; rather, I want to give you the information and present it to you in a simplified format where you can learn about it, and if it happens to be something that interests you, you'll be able to go back and do even more research independent and likely quicker than you could using a thick door-stopper book.

Action Steps

I. Create a personalized weblog style website using the resources I've directed you towards. Post a blog entry and become slightly familiar with the back office dashboard. It is fairly user friendly. Once you master blogging you'll be able to literally post blogs using your smartphone from anywhere you happen to be. I would encourage you to post ideas in the form of posts when they strike you. You never know when an idea will strike so it is a good idea to keep your smartphone with you. Also blogging an idea will also ensure you don't forget it. Keep in mind you can also benefit from later reading your own blog entries.

II. Create an integrated marketing communications plan (IMC). You'll need to definitely set up social media accounts that represent your personal branding. You'll also want to utilize some software that will help you measure the IMC.

CHAPTER 6

Direct Selling

Selling is something I've done all my life professionally in some capacity or other. This being said not everybody feels expert, self-assured, or adept to sell.

I was involved with a network marketing company about seven years ago or so. The company's system was setup to where you IBOs had to call back leads and sell them on the opportunity. The payoff was a minimum of $1000 straight commission when someone joined. As a sales guy I loved this particular opportunity and did quite well.

One day though I recruited a guy who was super nice and pleasant to deal with and I was figuring he'd be an excellent IBO on my down-line. A day after I recruited him he called me up and I was expecting him to tell me he made his first sale. Instead he was calling me up to tell me this opportunity wasn't right for him and could he have a refund. My jaw dropped! But, not because he wanted a refund; rather, because he told me in during the conversation that he was deathly afraid to call on leads. He said he tried and hung the phone up before the lead even answered.

It was one of the first, but definitely not the last time, I had a new IBO call me and tell me they couldn't sell to save their life.

If this is you, I have good news for you! You can sell, and you can sell well; however, you need to learn how to sell and exactly what selling is in network marketing.

I know…I know…but, please, trust me on this, and suspend your disbelief until you hear me out. Promise me at least that you'll keep an open mind.

Why Direct Selling?

Direct selling is something you'll only ever get better at. It's sort of the same with any network marketing business you start—you'll only continue to get more proficient and make more income as time goes by.

This should bring a smile to your face, since you now are getting started in a new business and learning new skills that will only continue to increase your wealth. I think this is pretty empowering in and of itself.

One of the things you can be assured of with selling is you'll never have to worry about a glass ceiling looming overhead acting as a cap on your salary. Sales people generally earn more income than just about any other profession. I want you to think about selling a little different than you may have in the past. We all know small business owners who have opened up shop wanting to expand their potential to make money. I mean just look in the mirror at yourself. You're not the proud owner of your very own business. Now ask yourself what is the purpose of a business? Is it to give away goods and products or to sell them? Obvious, right?

Congratulations you're a legitimately approved sales professional. In this business, like any other, you'll be selling. I might would go so far as to argue that anytime we ask for something and get what we want we're selling.

What is Direct Selling?

Direct selling is the marketing and selling of products away from a fixed location. In other words, you're peddling products to people directly.

According to the World Federation of Direct Selling Associations (WFDSA) 114 billion dollars in sales were achieved through the efforts of 62 million independent business owners, like yourself. The population of the United States here in 2014 is estimated to be around 317 million. There's a whole lot of us IBOs out here, wouldn't you agree?

I always find it interesting when people tell me nobody wants to buy what they have to sell. 114 billion dollars in one year just from those affiliated with WFDSA is a whole lot of nothing—not!

The truth is most people like to buy nice things whether they admit it or not. I mean who doesn't want to buy something if they have the money to purchase it and they desire to possess it?

The problem with most people who get started in the direct selling network marketing industry is they are either selling to the wrong market, i.e. not their target market, or they simply don't know how to sell, because nobody's ever taught them.

How to Sell Network Marketing

Selling a business opportunity is as simple as following a few simple steps:

I.   Prospect leads from your target market. This can be done through advertising and marketing efforts.

II.   Call on leads to build rapport, discover problems your product can resolve or be the answer to, and then present your sales proposal to the potential customer, emphasizing how your product will help them alleviate the problem they've told you they have.

III. Overcome objections.

IV.   Close the sale.

I want you to understand that this is a very traditional approach to selling. It is the one most new salespeople will have learnt most likely on the job. There are, in my opinion, approaches that work better than this one when selling network marketing.

Personally I use a question-based hypnotic selling approach. Please refer to my book: "Question-Based Hypnotic Selling" to learn more about this approach and in complete detail. You'll most likely have much better results over this traditional approach and you'll feel more confident and enjoy selling much better.

What if You Use a Different Method?

Using a different method you're more comfortable with really makes no difference, since what's ultimately important are the results you achieve in the end.

I've seen network marketers sell their business opportunities using methods that made me cringe and say to myself, "I'll never sell like that," and make tons of successful sales. I've also seen people use the traditional approach I've taught you here and have great results. So as far as utilizing any particular method my advice is to use the one that feels right to you and works.

I think selling, once practiced enough, becomes something of a rather unconscious act. With practice I believe most anyone will sell without realizing their selling someone something.

Just be ethical, stay within the bounds of the law, and do not make promises you cannot keep. I also prefer to be upfront and honest about my company and product's limitations. I want people to know full well what to expect and what my company is all about, and me of course.

Overall if you treat people fairly and kindly they'll reciprocate and do the same back to you. If you try and force someone to do something that isn't right or comfortable to them then you're setting yourself up for failure.

Just think if you have to hard sell someone into joining your network marketing team, they're probably thinking less of you, and less of your company, because they're likely thinking, if not consciously at least unconsciously, that they'll have to do the same thing. I'm going to suggest to you that a lot of people will be turned off from this hard sell approach.

Chapter Summary & End Note Commentary

In this chapter you learned how to sell according to the traditional and most commonly used method. You've also learned that selling is something you do all the time without consciously considering yourself doing it. You've also learned that you should always treat others the way you expect to be treated yourself—the Golden Rule!

The main point I want to bring home is the idea that selling can be a natural extension of yourself and you will only get better the longer you are in direct sales.

I've always looked at selling as helping people solve a problem or find an answer to some drawback they might be experiencing. In network marketing the primary drawbacks most people will express they have are: (a) the desire to work from home and not have to no longer punch a time card, (b) they want more time to spend with family and to be able to do more of what they want out of life, and (c) they want to be able to work from anywhere and earn a substantial income that will support the lifestyle vision they have in their head they want.

Chances are if you are honest with yourself you'll realize that one of these three or more than one of these is perhaps why you decided to get started in a new business opportunity that you truly believe will be your out from having to work for someone else or some company you cannot get behind anymore.

We sell ourselves, don't we?!! I mean, to be honest, I sold myself into joining a network marketing company, because I wanted to be able to work from anywhere I chose.

As a child my older brother used to pick-up from the local grocery store these work-from-home magazines. He'd skim through them, and then toss them haphazardly on the coffee-table. I spent a lot of hours bored as a child, so I would pick them up and read what they had to offer. I was magnetized to the mystery and how easy it seemed to be able to accomplish, what in my mind, I think I always wished for.

As I got older I wasn't really ever passionate about any job I did. People would ask me, "What do you want to do with your life?" My answer would often shock them: "I just want to be able to work-from-home and do as little as possible."

Now as I reflect back to this answer, I realize that doing very little is a poor waste of value and doesn't promote the personal brand I want to promote.

Today, I am doing what I always wanted; however, I'm passionately providing as much value as possible to others.

> *"If you can dream it, then you can achieve it. You will get all you want in life if you help enough other people get what they want." —Zig Zigglar*

Action Steps

The following action steps are designed to help you learn how to sell better. The problem with most people is they will read it in a book or hear it from a friend, but when it comes time to put into practice, or implement, or apply what it is they have learnt, they won't.

My experiences in network marketing, and as a professional sales trainer, has taught me all too well that you can lead a horse to water, but you can't make him drink. Simply put: If you do not use what you learn and make it useful it will always remain useless for you and you'll never know the true value of what you've learnt.

This is one reason why some of you reading this book will go on to be highly successful and get everything you want out of the network marketing industry and others will fail and blame others for why you can't have what it is you want. In persuasion psychology they call this phenomenon: Attribution Theory. It explains the phenomenon that happens when we take credit for things inwardly claiming we achieved such-and-such goal because of our awesome education and ability to lead armies into battle; but when something happens to cause up to slip up or perform poorly, we'll simply blame it on some external cause, like: "My dog ate my homework!" Attribution Theory explains why we take credit for things and blame others when things don't go so well. My advice to you is to hold yourself accountable and take responsibilities for your wins but also your losses. I don't truthfully believe in failure or loss; I believe in feedback. If it weren't for all the times I failed at network marketing I wouldn't be able to write this book for you today. I had to step into your shoes first, before you, so that I could be able to help you. In selling you might want to approach your potential customers from this same perspective. Get in their shoes, understand their unique situations, and support them and problem solve with them, and you'll come up with some great solutions and answers that will no-less help them get started in your network marketing business—they'll love you for your willingness to understand and help them. This will make you a leader.

I. Read both: "Secret Sales Hypnosis" and "Question-Based Hypnotic Selling". Both of these books will give you much more information on alternative sales processes so you can discover which method most in alignment with your personality and predilection. You'll also learn some really amazing tips and secrets that will lessen the learning curve for you when it comes to direct selling others into your network marketing business.

II.   Record in summary what you've learned about selling in general. Talk about how you felt about selling and salespeople personally. Talk about the sales process that makes the most sense to you. Then transcribe your recording into a Word document and save both the audio and Word document into your Network Marketing folder.

III.   Practice calling on some people whom you think are in your target market. Tell them who you are and be friendly, and most importantly listen 90% of the time. People love to talk about themselves. If you make a sale, fine; if you don't make a sale, fine. Just practice sharing your new opportunity with individuals you think it might help. Always, before you hang-up the phone, or part company, ask for the sale. This is as simple as asking: "I have to ask you. Will you join my team and get started with me today?" Once you ask this, say nothing until after they give you an answer. In sales, every seasoned sales professional knows, "The person who speaks first after a sale has been asked for, loses." This simply means that if you ask them to join, and then sense their hesitation and so decide to say something else to help push them over the fence to say yes, they'll almost always invariably tell you "No." You have to learn to shut-up when you ask for the sale—it is imperative to your success!

CHAPTER 7

Monetize Everything

In this chapter we'll look at ways you can monetize all of your daily activities; explicitly, to put more money into your pocket at the end of every day. You'll learn about the importance of charging a price for your time. You'll learn about the importance of resource management. You'll learn how to put many of the tools I've required you to possess as a prerequisite for this course and how to make money utilizing them effectively-well.

You must start to understand the importance of time management and realize when you own a business you'll often times feel more married to it than your spouse. If you're not married you'll feel like you have even less time than you did when you were working that 9 – 5 job; namely, for the reasons you could dissociate yourself from your job once you left the office at the end of your shift. In a network marketing business things can get a little challenging with having to juggle so much coming from you at all directions.

You'll have people calling you at the weirdest times of day and night if you're not careful in your planning. You'll have loved ones you live with criticizing you for not spending your waking hours at home with them; not able to understand that just because you're no longer working an outside job, that you are still working, and need time, space, and quiet, away from them, to make this new network marketing gig work. I mean, think about it, 'work' is in the name of the industry you're now a part of.

You'll also experience mood shifts happening when others in your network send you over email, ring you up, or Skype you or FB message you about the problems their continuing to experience, or unable to overcome without your help. These emotions will be anger, fear, discouragement, negativity, and more. If your up-line leader required you to own this book and read it in its entirety one reason is because they didn't have the heart to tell you to quit bothering them with all of life's problems.

What they want to say to you but don't have the heart to say is, "Get over yourself! Go meditate or something! Talk to a priest, a bishop, a rabbi, or some other spiritual pundit. Quit calling all the time. Quite emailing so much. Quit making excuses. Start making sales calls and doing more prospecting. And if you must call only call me to inform me you've made a sale or recruited someone new into the down-line." You see, your up-line leader does care about you, treasures your friendship, and values you as a member of the team; however, they're busy making money, recruiting new people, and growing their business—they certainly don't have time to spend on the phone with you all day talking about how bad you got it, or how stressed out you are at your job. The answer you must come face-to-face with is that you are the answer to your problem. If you want to make more money, then you must take the necessary actions to make more money.

Nobody is going to throw you a bone, without expecting you to reciprocate, pay them for the bone, or kick them back some commissions when you finally pick-up the bone and find that it is actually a new recruit you've gained and not a bone, per se.

Why Monetize Everything

Everything has value and therefore has a price tag attached. When we're born into this world we enter with nothing, including clothes. Everything we achieve, are given, or earn, after this entrance into the world has a value associated to it.

The clothes you're wearing right now have a value. The book you're reading right now also has a value. The time you're taking to read this book also has a value. The point is everything, regardless of what you might think or not, has some type of value attached to it. For this reason you must learn to start getting paid for the value you are freely handing over to others, which you've been conditioned and led to believe has no value. I'm here to tell you it and everything else in this world has value.

If you don't ask for the sale the potential customer likely won't buy what you're offering them. You must ask for the sale, because what you want is one thing in exchange for giving something else up that also has value. If you *give away things of value* you're telling other people, and yourself, that the things you're giving away have zero value. Whatever you ask for something in terms of price is what you are self-declaring the value of the thing is worth to you. People hence will take their idea of what it is worth and compare it with your idea and then negotiate the price with you from that perspective.

In the olden days people relied on the barter system. This is when one person, let's say they're excellent at making bread, would trade their bread for something else they needed—for example, they might trade their bread to the person down the road who makes bread-pans.

How many loaves of bread to you think the bread maker must trade to the bread-pan maker in order to get a new bread pan?

If you ask this question to ten people they'll all give you a different answer most likely. This is why it is important to realistically state the value an item possesses as you see it having. People will invariably disagree about price, because everybody buying something wants it for less, while everybody selling something wants more for it. It's the nature of selling.

Why you need to monetize everything is because it will increase your value and decrease the number of occurrences when people call you up wanting something for nothing. Remember, 'nothing' has zero value, and in fact is usually perceived as being cheap or worthless. In people's minds it is worthless.

If you believe that you're not worthless I suggest you learn the art and get in the habit of monetizing everything you do from this point on in your network marketing career.

What Can You Monetize?

You can literally monetize everything in my opinion. You can monetize your time; charging people for your consulting services. You can monetize what you know; creating information products or courses around what you know. You can monetize your services; charging you new recruits when they ask you to go back in their back office to resize a website banner in Photoshop. You can monetize your vacations; that is, you can use them as opportunities to increase the value of your personal brand by shooting on your smartphone YouTube.com videos.

I'm going to let you in on a little secret. I've been in network marketing for many years. I know everything I'm teaching you to do in this book both backwards and forwards. I've spent countless hours on the phone training new recruits. I've made screencast videos to teach what I know to people in my down line. I've wasted hours of my life doing many of these activities simply because I didn't charge money when I should have. I am guilty, you might say, of devaluing myself in this industry. What was my number one excuse, and probably will be yours too? My number one excuse was I'm a nice guy and I truly care and I wanted to help people become as successful as I am, so I freely gave away my value.

What did it cost me besides lots of money? It cost me my and self-worth—more valuable to me than the money! I was just talking to one of my down line members on the phone, about an hour ago. He wanted me to help him cut his photo out and paste in onto a background using my expertise in graphic design. I told me I usually charge $100 to do that, but since he's a friend and in my down line I'd only charge him $50.

There was a pause, a very long pause, and then finally he said, "Okay, can I PayPal you the money?" I told him, "Sure. We'll process that right now and I'll have it to you by the end of the day." He paid, I took 10 minutes of my time creating the banner, sent it to him, and he loved it. Why? Because there was value attached to the work I did for him. Had I done it for free he would have felt indebted to me most likely, but also likely not perceived the value in my craftsmanship.

This is just another example of something you can monetize. Like I say though, you can monetize everything, and you should in my opinion.

How to Monetize Everything

Monetizing everything must become a ritual habit. Chances are you're in the habit of doing most everything in your life for free. I changed my mindset about my value when I heard a speaker give an interview once.

He said he had a client who wanted to book him for a keynote speech. The speaker only had $2000 to pay him. He said he would do it for no less than $5000. They told him they'd have to think about it. He told them, take the rest of your life to decide, the price won't go down; however, I can't guarantee it won't go up.

He later revealed that the events manager called him in hours not days and booked him at the rate he quoted them. He also said, and I never forgot this, "I won't put a suit on for less than the cost of the suit." At the time I was thinking about a conversation with a girl I had earlier that week. She was telling me that she had to buy her own uniform at the fast-food restaurant she was employed to. This got me thinking a lot about value and peoples' perceptions. The poor girl working at a fast-food restaurant had to not only buy her uniform, but pay money each week to wash it, then spend time bathing and grooming herself before and after going to work, and then, as if that wasn't costly enough, she had to go to a job that barely paid her a living wage, and then get ordered around all day. What is she saying about her value? What habits have you absorbed from the beliefs you've formed in your mind?

The good news is you can stop these beliefs from devaluing you and your lifestyle. The guy who won't put on a suit until he's paid at least what the cost of the suit is valued at truly understands his value. He's probably, and I think you'll agree, making more money per year than the girl who has to pay for her ugly fast-food uniform just to work a job she doesn't exactly enjoy.

So let's look at the resources you already own, which are at your disposal. Let me teach you some ways you can monetize from them.

I.   Laptop: Your laptop can be used in a number of ways to land you some fast cash. You can use it to write articles for other network marketers and charge for them. You can write a book and sell it much the same way I have done writing this one. You can do graphic art work. You can tutor people online through sites like: tutor.com, and you can do an unlimited number of other tasks using nothing more than your laptop.

II.   Wacom Tablet: You can use this tablet device to create graphic designs, which you can sell to those in your down line. You can also use it to create sales copy graphics to use on your own website as well as sell to other internet marketers. You can also use it to create screencast videos using screen capture software like Camtasia . These videos can then be sold to those in your down line or else to others interested in knowing about something you already know quite well

III.   In time, if not already, you'll have a working knowledge of Adobe's CC Suite of products. These software will allow you to create e-books, newsletters, templates, graphics, videos, and a whole host of other information products you can sell directly to your down line or other markets.

IV.   Microsoft Office 365 will be useful for creating and editing documents. It is also worth mentioning that you'll be able to take advantage of many free templates available through the Microsoft.com website. These can be used to keep track of accounts, as well as track your progress and your business growth. In fact, you'll be able to find a template on there that can be used as a DMO plan calendar. It can be printed off on a single page, and using a punch-hole make it so you can easily insert it into a binder. This way you can keep notes about upcoming appointments and be able to go back and look to see what you did even days earlier in your business. You can also create personalized templates for Word, Excel, and PowerPoint which can be sold to your down line or to sell on your personally branded website as an instant download.

V.   H1 Zoom: This is one of my most used tools in my business. I use it to create audio downloads which I sell on www.indirectknowledge.com and which I also use to record live workshops I present at in combination with my Sony Erickson EMC CSC Lapel Mic. What I do is attach the microphone to my H1 Zoom and then slip the zoom into my pocket while I'm lecturing and educating an audience. When finished, this audio can be edited using Adobe's Audition (in-cluded in the Adobe CC Suite) for selling in the form of CD's and MP3 downloads. You can also have the audio transcribed using your Express Scribe and offer put into a book format or e-book format and sell the complete training over and over again.

VI. Dragon Naturally Speaking: This is another great program which can be used to talk out your audio recordings for the purpose of easier transcribing. It can also be useful for writing and sending out emails much quicker, saving you precious time.

VII. Skype Headset/Skype: Using Skype and your headset you can download software online that will let you record both yourself and someone else whom you're communicating with via Skype. This will be saved in an MP4 video format. You can then go back and edit using Adobe's Premier Pro (included in Adobe's CC Suite) and the sold through various channels. It can also be a great training tool, which you can have transcribed into a Word document and then after transcribing/editing you can save it as a PDF, which can then be hosted on your website as an instant download product.

VIII.   SmartPhone: A modern day smartphone opens up many channels of communication for you. If you're not always able to be at your home office or take your laptop to a nearby coffeehouse, an internet ready smartphone will allow you to write blog articles, promoting your business opportunity, while also helping you to brand yourself, and your business. It can also be used to write emails, communicate through social media channels, and you can also download a Skype Application that allows you to keep in touch via Skype with other IBO's. You can create videos using your SmartPhone which can be sold online as well.

These tools I've mentioned are only some of the ones I required you to own. Many of these tools can be used together to create some pretty amazing and high quality information products. They are tools that you can also easily learn to use, and in my opinion are fun to learn.

What if You Come Up With Other Ideas?

The sky really is the limit in terms of how you can and might apply these tools in ways to generate consistent and regular income from everything you do in your business.

Something I didn't mention, but that I often refer new IBOs in my down line to pursue, especially those who have went against my advice and quit their jobs, or those who were jobless when they got started with me, and that's freelance marketplaces. These are sites like: www.odesk.com, www.freelancer.com, www.guru.com, www.peopleperhour.com, www.elance.com, and www.fiverr.com. The tools you already have at your disposal can be used to generate some fairly consistent income doing jobs from home for others. You will need to take the time on some of these sites to take skill tests, and some will require a portfolio. Regardless if you are required to have a portfolio or not, you'll be able to after a few jobs you do, put together a decent portfolio to help you land more jobs. A last benefit is the experience you get in doing such jobs will help you in the future as you grow your business, and the best part is you'll be monetizing your training.

Sometimes I still do freelance for fun and to hone my own skills. I encourage you to do the same.

Chapter Summary & End Note Commentary

In this chapter we looked at the idea of monetizing your time and skillsets to produce larger amounts of income, while also increasing your personal value.

Most people are unaware of their true value in the marketplace and so this chapter has been provided to get you thinking about how you can increase your value and make more money in the process, while also saving yourself time and headaches.

Your training should be paid, just like if you worked for a company having to learn new systems, procedures, policies, and skills. Unfortunately most people new to network marketing aren't thinking enough about how to make money learning how to make money. Your up line isn't going to come off of any money; however, they'll expect you to pull your weight and work hard to make them more money. Your ever increasing down line will be seeking your advice, trying to rob you of your time that you should be spending working your own business.

The major problem I've noticed in the network marketing industry is that those above you want for you to just 'get it' on your own and rely on the company training. The company training is most often designed to help the organization pull in more recruits from you in as quick a time frame as possible; for the reason they don't anticipate you sticking around long. So they're trying to get as much of your money and your personal resources as possible before you bail out of the industry; and, broker than you were before you came in.

You, as a new recruit, are seriously excited and wanting to make a fast buck quicker than humanly possible, yet you lack the proper training, and you're likely like most—you're needy! This means you want to talk one-on-one with your up line like they're some type of customer service expert whose only purpose on this planet is to help you build your own business.

As a business owner it is time to grow up, and face responsibilities. You'll work hard, and consistently, but you'll always be making more and more income. One day you'll likely wake-up with the thought that you've just pulled in a $20,000 month, and realize that this is more money than you pulled in during an entire year of killing yourself working for the man at some 9 – 5 job. At this point you'll never look back and will feel as though you've accomplished some great feat of magic, only a powerful sorcerer could pull off—and you'd be right to think this!

Action Steps

I.   Record into you H1 Zoom all the insights you've received from reading this chapter. Think first about how these tools and your time matters and how from this moment on you'll monetize everything that you do. Like before in other chapters, transcribe the audio and save it in your Network Marketing folder.

II.   While you're in your Network Marketing folder I want you to rename all the audio files as "Module 1," "Module 2," etc. Do the same for the Word documents and save them as a PDF file. After you've done this I want you to visit: https://sellfy.com/ and sell them on this site, any others you can find, as well as on your personally branded website. You can label the audio course anything you like, but I would recommend something similar to: "Network Marketing Success Formula" or the like.

III.   From this point forward whenever you recruit someone new into your organization I want you to require them to purchase this book either through www.indirectknowledge.com or else through www.amazon.com. Assure them that this book will help them with getting started in this industry. What this will do for you is dissociate them away from you, allowing you to work your business and continue monetizing your efforts—all leading to greater sustained growth for your business, but also theirs as well. By referring them to this book it takes the pressure off of you having to explain everything they need to know. It also shows that you're not just trying to make a quick buck off of them trying to get them to purchase your products, etc. Trust and integrity and maintaining your own personal brand should never come by way of trying to make a quick buck off of your new recruit.

The purpose of creating an audio and digital document was for a couple reasons; namely, I wanted you to do it to learn how easy it is to create an information product that you will be able to sell forever and ever online while only having to do the work once ever, I also wanted to make you your money back from the purchase of this book by proving the value of this book to you, I also wanted you to have a product on your personally branded website for those not quite sold on your opportunity to be able to buy to learn more about you, and to prove that you're a leader in this industry that they can look up to. Never sell your digital product to your down line. This will hinder them from gaining complete trust in you. Also, and this is really important: If you try and sell it to them they likely will not buy it anyway. If you have it on your website and they see it, their curiosity will likely get the best of them and they will have to purchase it. Lastly, after you have referred them to this book, they'll likely visit your website to see how seriously you took this course, and in order to find out, they'll have to purchase it from you.

Duplication is EVERYTHING in network marketing. The example you set for others will be the example they set for others they will recruit. Your integrity, personal brand, and business are at stake, and the easiest way to crumble your empire is deviate from this plan.

References

Griffiths, A., & Toms, W. (2008). *101 ways to build a successful network marketing business.* Crows Nest, NSW: Allen & Unwin.

Rubino, J., & Terhune, J. (2006). *15 secrets every network marketer must know: Essential elements and skills required to achieve 6- & 7-figure success in network marketing.* Hoboken, N.J.: John Wiley & Sons.

Christensen, M. (2007). *Be a network marketing superstar: The one book you need to make more money than you ever thought possible.* New York: AMACOM.

Christensen, M. (2008). *Be a recruiting superstar: The fast track to network marketing millions.* New York: American Management Association.

Adler, J. (2012). *Beach money: Creating your dream life through network marketing* (2nd ed.). Salt Lake City, UT: Eagle One Pub., LLC.

Connor, T. (2000). *52 network marketing tips for success, wealth and happiness.* Mechanicsburg, PA: Executive Books.

Kalench, J. (1990). *Being the best you can be in MLM: How to train your way to the top in multi-level/network marketing--America's fastest-growing industry.* Encinitas, CA: MIM Publications.

Go, J. (2000). *Build, grow and sustain your network marketing distributor business.* Quezon City, Philippines: Design Plus.

Moore, A. L. (1998). *Building a successful network marketing company: The systems, the products, and the know-how you need to launch or enhance a successful MLM company.* Rocklin, CA: Prima Pub.

Berry, R. (1997). *Direct selling: From door to door to network marketing.* Boston: Butterworth-Heinemann.

Fox, S. C. (2012). *Click millionaires: Work less, live more with an internet business you love.* New York: American Management Association.

Tribble, T. (Ã2012). *Double your income with network marketing: Create financial security in just minutes a day...without quitting your job.* Hoboken, New Jersey: John Wiley & Sons, Inc.

DeGarmo, S., & Tartaglia, L. A. (1999). *Heart to heart: The real power of network marketing.* Rocklin, Calif.: Prima Pub.

Halls, K. (2011). *From millions to millions and millions more!: The 9 rules to succeed in network marketing.* Washington, DC.

Keefe, C. R. (2009). *How bad do you want it ?: Achieve your needs, gain access to your wants with network marketing.* Laguna Hills, California: Apriori Press.

Gage, R. (1998). *How to build a multi-level money machine: The science of network marketing.* Miami Beach, Fla.: GR&DI Publications.

Yarnell, M. (2012). *How to become filthy, stinking rich through network marketing: Without alienating friends and family.* Hoboken, N.J.: John Wiley & Sons.

Ziglar, Z. (2001). *Network marketing for dummies.* Foster City, CA: IDG Books Worldwide.

Clements, L. W. (2000). *Inside network marketing: An expert's view into the hidden truths and exploited myths of America's most misunderstood industry* (Rev. and updated 2nd ed.). Roseville, CA: Prima Pub.

Spirer, G. (2011). *Quick steps to network marketing success: Dare to dream huge.* Garden City, VA: Morgan James Pub., LLC.

Paley, R. (2000). *Russ Paley's ultimate guide to network marketing: Your step-by-step guide to wealth.* Franklin Lakes, NJ: Career Press.

Rubino, J. (2004). *Secrets of building a million dollar network marketing organization: From a guy who's been there, done that, and shows you how you can do it too.* Boxford, MA: Vision Works Pub. (Reprinted from 2004th ed.).

Index

ABOUT THE AUTHOR

Bryan Westra is a successful network marketer who has been in the industry for 15+ years. He holds an MBA in Marketing and is a PH.D. Candidate in Counseling. He is also founder and lead trainer at Indirect Knowledge Limited. www.indirectknowledge.com

www.ingramcontent.com/pod-product-compliance
Lightning Source LLC
Chambersburg PA
CBHW031811190326
41518CB00006B/290